T0354619

THE ABC'S OF
EDUCATION:
EURO-AMERICAN STYLE

An Alternative Approach to Education

SUZANNE ZURILGEN STRAUSS

authorHOUSE®

AuthorHouse™
1663 Liberty Drive
Bloomington, IN 47403
www.authorhouse.com
Phone: 1-800-839-8640

Published by AuthorHouse   08/13/2012

ISBN: 978-1-4670-6111-7 (sc)

CONTENTS

PREFACE

My education all started the day I went to an interview for a teaching job. I was living on unemployment and making more money than the job was to pay. I had a Bachelor's Degree from U.C. Berkeley, no teaching experience or certification, but I thought that teaching might be rather interesting. I had nothing to lose. I was a Toastmaster, so I didn't fear the interview, which was before four other teachers and the principal. So, I marched in there, expecting to have a little fun since speaking in front of groups was my forte. The lady who was before me came out in tears. I was still undaunted. I confidently walked in, sat down, smiled at all of them and waited for the barrage of questions. Well, of course, the way a group interview works is for everyone to get their two cents' worth in at my expense. When the teachers started to ask me what I would teach and how, I said I didn't know because I had never taught before, nor did I have any prior classes in education. So, I turned the interview around and I began to interview them. What do you teach? What methods do you use? How do you deal with discipline? That was at 3:30 pm on a Thursday. At 5 pm that day, the principal called and asked if I wanted the job. He said come in on Friday and observe, pick up the textbooks, and then be ready to teach on Monday. However, the job was conditional.

In order to qualify to teach, I had to get my certification while I taught. This was a small New Hampshire mill town called Newmarket. I was to teach four classes for $4500.00 a year. I was in full agreement as I liked going to college and enjoyed learning. So, I started teaching school and taking classes the following Monday. However, nothing prepared me for the first detention I gave. The student stood up, took the detention, looked at it, stared at me, and gobbled up the slip of paper, right before my very eyes! I just stood there, wondering if all students ate their detentions. That was just the beginning of a trial by fire (literally and figuratively). It was later that year, that a student set fire to my room to protest my mean-spirited ways as a teacher. That began a search for the ideal education. My search is ongoing and this book is about my search for a way to reach kids and remain sane as a teacher.

"The journey of a thousand miles begins with one step", as Lao Tse, a Chinese philosopher once said. Just so, I began twenty-two years ago to chart the waters of my endless journey into the depths of the vast ocean of academia. I still hope to discover who I am and where I fit in, in this miasmic sea of education. I use the ocean as a motif for learning, for as vast as the sea is, so also are the different systems of education in America and elsewhere.

As part of this journey, I spent 22 years teaching in American high schools, and the year (98-99) in a German Gesamtschule (the "equivalent" of our high school). I spent a year as an exchange student at a German university, and three other years living in Austria, Germany, and Switzerland. I have a good understanding for the European educational system.

I have also taught on both the East and the West Coast, from schools with 50 in a graduating class to 750. I have used varied methods. Some examples are: Tech Prep, Career Pathways, School to Career, and Communication 2000 (all basically different names for approximately the same school-to-work philosophy for the other-than-traditional-college-committed kid). College prep and GATE (for advanced learners) were the other side of that coin. I have piloted new programs, watched de-tracking derail, led seminars and workshops, spoke in conferences, written grants and received funds to do innovative and new programs. These "terrific" programs were designated by the federal or state government as being the latest, greatest "special project". Then watched them crash and burn because funds ran out. I have team taught, shuttled back and forth between two school sites, been shafted, shifted and set adrift on the shores of Education Never Never Land, and now I embark on yet another journey . . . to write about my experiences and try to make some sense of this confusion we call American education. With a European perspective, I will develop the best of both worlds, by outlining the best of both educational systems. To balance this rather serious subject, I will insert poetry to light the way to a different paradigm shift. What programs are better, how are they instituted, and where can they be rearranged to enhance the educational experience? That part of the study will presently unfold.

ACKNOWLEDGEMENTS

I will be eternally grateful to my husband, Martin, who has stood behind me in every endeavor I have ever attempted in my life. He is my rock, my biggest fan, my greatest supporter. Thank you, Schatz!

I would also like to thank Renate Schneider from Bruehl, Germany, who was also an English teacher in her own country, and helped me to keep the details accurate about the German school system. She proofread my manuscript twice for me and continues to be a great support. Thank you, Renate!

ACCLIMATION
GETTING MY FEET WET

Getting acclimated to a new teaching environment in a foreign country is not exactly like riding a gentle wave, especially when the tides are so strange. There are many considerations. The memories of the first few days/weeks arriving at my destination can be found in the APPENDIX (if you wish to travel with me on a step-by-step journey). Otherwise, these were some of my general observances.

The question always comes up . . . should a 50-year-old married woman, who has an excellent relationship with her husband, leave home for a whole year to pursue an old dream? The answer to that question lies in two things. How good of a marriage does she have and how flexible is she?

Number one, how good is her marriage. On the one hand, her relationship is so strong and so good that her husband agrees to an arrangement of a complete stranger living with him for a year, so she can fulfill her dream. He finds her dream to be so important that he wants her to be happy and sublimates his feelings for the sake of hers. She knows what a sacrifice it is and really appreciates the fact that he is so willing to let her take this step. On the other hand, the relationship is so good that being without her husband is extremely painful. Only she does not realize this until she is away from him for two months. Then she begins to cry and feel like she can't control herself another minute without him. So, having a good marriage is a double-edged sword. There is so much trust that the spouse is willing to let her go away, yet the going away is painful due to the relationship's fine nature. She had everything to gain professionally and everything to lose personally.

Number two: flexibility. Being a 50 year old woman, she is used to her husband, who takes care of her every need. He provides her with expensive Mercedes Benz's, leaves 100 dollar bills on the dresser for her, maintains her cars, pays the bills, makes sure she has a cell phone and plenty of charge cards, a housekeeper, gardener, trips to Europe, new houses, and worries about every little aspect of her life. Suddenly, this middle-aged woman is on her own. She can no longer rely on someone else to do everything for her. She is forced to find a used car, pay all the bills, buy all the groceries, do her own cleaning, run her own errands, fix her own car and entertain herself. That's a tall order for a 50-year-old happily married woman.

Getting used to a new environment at this age is like driving a two-ton truck down an L.A. freeway! It isn't easy! Furthermore, it isn't much fun. What happened to the carefree life of weekending at the beach? Every weekend going to Pacific Grove, Carmel, Monterey, walking the dog on the beach, taking in a new restaurant, shopping in some new funky shop, grabbing a bowl of chowder at our favorite chowder restaurant, taking a sunset drive, and breezing down to the water, lying open faced in the sun.

I gave it all up to be in a wet, cold, damp, dreary Northern German town with two mangy cats that pee in my bathroom and a neurotic dog that thinks I am one of his personal tormentors. Living with someone else's droopy plants, and wigged out carpet and funky pictures and do-dads cluttering up the place. And what did I leave behind? Antique sideboards and elegant dressers, a canopied bed traded in for a waterbed, my lovely fainting couch for a hideabed, my crystal glasses for flea market crockery, my Benz for a antiquated VW, my furs and jewels for a loose sweater and jeans.

So, next time you think of leaving home, ask yourself how much you will miss your darling husband and how flexible you really are, then ask yourself if it is worth giving up a year of your life for a dream. A far-fetched dream that might turn into a formidable nightmare! However, you know what? If I had it to do all over again, I would do it in a heartbeat. It taught me many things, besides my inability to do the things I did when I was twenty. It reminded me that I am self-sufficient, still able to take care of myself. It reinforced my sense of adventure, and left me with a longing to return. However, it can be a real test for your marriage. Unfortunately, the worst of the arrangement is always whether you can get along with the housemate that ends up sharing your space. With my husband, he had his housemate across the hall from him and they shared the whole house. I had an upstairs apartment that was completely for me alone.

I have to reiterate that the adventure was the essence of the experience. In my lifetime, I have had many experiences and it seems that this is what keeps me alive and vibrant. In fact, I am easily bored and this lends itself to changes I make in my curriculum, and the experiences I am able to share with my students. Life should be one enormous adventure, but kids don't see it that way, when all their experiences lead towards boredom if they are not engaged in something that excites them. This does not mean that we have to hearken back to the TV generation attitude that kids are used to being entertained. This may be part of it, but think about it for a moment. Do you enjoy things that have nothing to do with your true interests? Don't you get bored when exposed to daily routine that doesn't pertain to your own interests? If only kids could get their teeth into something that excites them; that stirs their imaginations! What a difference that would make. However, unless our attitudes change about the way we look at education, nothing in education will change for the better. Let us examine our attitudes.

ATTITUDES
EBB & FLOW

The core, the seed, the root of all-evil in education today has to be our attitudes. Why do parents want their children to have a college education? Shouldn't the consideration be that they have some kind of employable training or a college degree in a field of interest of their choice?

Why aren't these two goals in life equated with the same respect? What would the world be like if it was populated by only university-degreed people? I must quote one of my Berkeley professors I had long ago. He was a lawyer who taught classes at Berkeley and he was also revered by all of his students. He referred to his colleagues as "technically competent barbarians" and I really think he captured the essence of what it would be like to have a society run by these academic misfits. These intellectuals, so consumed with their ivory tower existence in academia that to ask him or her how to do a mundane task, would have required half a day in their study to decide just the right way to do it. For example, a PH.D may know the most minute details of the secretions of the African tsetse fly, but know little or nothing about the desires and needs of those kids who may be misplaced at the university. Of course, they expect the cream of the crop to have already been sorted through, if they are there in the first place. No, when it comes to handing over the day-to-day everyday routine of running the country, dealing with such mundane necessities as getting their toilets unplugged, forget it; the academicians will not be there to help. I know I sound angry about this segment of the population, but I am really trying to point out the need for more open-mindedness regarding all segments of the population. Academicians are important for their individual research in a variety of fields that enhance society, but it is not the only pathway to success.

Furthermore, ask yourself how much you pay your plumber for unplugging your toilet or how much you pay your mechanic to get that carburetor to work. You will generally find that they are making more money than an educator.

What is demeaning or embarrassing or inferior about making more money than a college professor? Then why do we continue to leave our young people uninformed about their total options? Why do we always have to couch it in terms of: Oh, well, if you can't go on to college, there is always working at McDonald's. I have a former student who started out frying French fries and worked himself up to manager and then bought his own franchise. Need I tell you how much more money he is making than me?

The sad part is that America offers technical schools of every variety and our junior colleges will allow you to pursue whatever trade you desire in half the time it takes to get a four year degree, but we are not collaborating with our local junior colleges, and that is the problem. Case in point. Another student of mine graduated from high school in 1996. His folks didn't have a lot of money to send him to university, so he went to our local junior college. He took a two year program in computer technology of some kind and landed a job in Silicon Valley, making $50,000 a year, starting pay. That's the kind of money I made after teaching for 20 years! I would say that is not so bad.

Now, let's take a look at what is expected in American schools. Since tracking students is a no-no nowadays for the sake of equality, we now have the "real" university bound kids in the GATE programs and the rest of the school thrown into a giant pot of stew. This stew is comprised of second grade readers with college level readers and everything in between, all in the same course, in the same class in high school. (I might add that the last school where I taught happened to be in a lower economic area where only 2% went directly to university.)

Given that only 2% go directly to university and these kids are covered in their GATE classes, why are we expecting everyone else to be college-bound and required to learn Shakespeare and Chaucer? Added to that are enormous class sizes (30-45) and added to that, the diversity in ability level and in ethnic background, and in mentality, and in perspective, and in motivation level, and in parental involvement (many parents don't speak English), and you have a pot of stew that's overflowing. When we finally turn the fire off, all we have left is soggy potatoes and tough meat! It just isn't working!

I call this sacrificing quality for the sake of equality. I call this educating the majority for the sake of the minority. You know who has the most say over educational matters in our society? Upper middle class parents. Parents who are educated themselves, who have lived in this country for several generations and know the system. Some parents may even be on the Board of Education and many of them may be friends of the Board members. Parents who know how to work the system. Parents who are advocates for superior education to benefit their little Johnny and Suzie. Parents who have a voice, who are assertive, who go to Open House, who attend the committee meetings, who are loud and aggressive and absolutely sure of what they want and they demand a superior education for their child. But when their children comprise a mere 2% of the total school population, how can this be representing the majority? Yes, we are expecting to churn out little intellectuals when a significant number cannot even read Dr. Seuss books, for heaven's sake! Shakespeare and Chaucer indeed!

As I mentioned before, our junior colleges do offer many fine programs where one can become certified in a trade. So why aren't we encouraging our students to pursue one of these fields and why isn't the high school giving them a chance to see what they like to do before they get entirely turned off to education and drop out and drop in to our local jails! According to a 2011 report, there is a 31% high school dropout rate, nationwide.

"Whites (23%); Hispanics (44%); Black (46%); Asian (19%); American Indian (49%)". Reasons for dropping out are:

Classes aren't interesting; parents/family/adults have low expectations; poor attendance; failing in school; family responsibilities (work, caring for siblings, etc.); becoming a parent; and too much freedom. Some of the warning signs are: they don't feel challenged in school; they don't feel high educational expectations from either their family or school; they believe their parents are too controlling and they want to rebel; they have trouble with schoolwork or feel like they are not as smart as other students; they have drug, alcohol or mental health problems; they regularly miss school or are frequently tardy; they struggle with problems at home, including physical or verbal abuse; they feel like they don't fit in or have friends at school; their peers or siblings have dropped out of school; or they have poor learning conditions at school—such as overcrowding, high levels of violence and excessive absenteeism (BoostUp.org Internet).

High schools need to provide a better selection of courses to accommodate the needs of every type of student. That's where Germany's system comes in.

The attitude in Germany is a much more realistic approach. Students are evaluated by their elementary school teacher, at the age of ten, and in consultation with the parents, teachers help decide which school that child should attend. Then either a vocational type school is made available, that leans more towards general studies or the college-bound high school is recommended. After the 6th and 10th grade, a child could be changed to another school system if he/she showed promise.

There are five types of schools in Germany. The Berufsschule, the Hauptschule, the Realschule, the Gymnasium, and the Gesamtschule. The Berufsschule is an apprenticeship program that requires 4 days of work at the place of employment and one full day of studies or 2 months of work and 1 month of schooling. The Hauptschule is grades 5-9 or 5-10, depending on the students' ability and motivation. The Realschule is a mixture of academically oriented classes, such as foreign languages and literature, and down-to-earth vocational training, especially from 7th to 9th grade on. Gymnasium is college-bound, with rigorous academic courses in preparation for university. The Gesamtschule (which translates to "together school") combines some of all these schools in one school system. It has 5th through 9th or 10th grades, which are required and 11th through 13th grades, which are optional.

There is still some stigma attached to technical education as opposed to college education, but it is far less pronounced in Europe and does not have the sense of failure that we impart to our kids if they choose not to go to college.

Children always ask why they must learn something and if they find it meaningless, they will not learn and they become totally turned off to education. "Give a man a fish and he eats for one day, but teach him how to fish and he eats for life." It doesn't matter what a child pursues, only that he/she is content in that endeavor, and that he/she is using that God-given gift to its best advantage. But how can a child know where his gift lies if we don't open the doors and let them explore what is behind them? Have a look at what Germany's programs offer.

Fulbright Evaluation & Reflections

My decision to apply for the Fulbright Teacher Exchange Program was involved with my future exchange partner contacting me by e-mail and asking if I was interested in getting involved. I had attended an e-mail project seminar in Hamburg and Berlin a few years before, and my partner got my e-mail address from one of his colleagues who also attended that seminar.

Since we both corresponded for a year prior to our exchange, there was plenty of time to get to know him and get acquainted with his school. However, it did not fully prepare him for the bigger shock of class sizes and rules and regulations quite different from the German system. In spite of the fact that I told him all these things ahead of time, he was still very disappointed and disillusioned.

I feel that it was easier for me because I went from a difficult situation to a much easier one. In Germany, they are so much more realistic in terms of what they expect from their teachers and they provide plenty of opportunities to support the teacher in the classroom. In my school, here in the Central Valley in California, we have several things that complicate the situation. Some of those problems are enormous class sizes: 35-45 in English classes, sophomore through senior. Major multi-cultural differences in background, ability levels, economic levels, and attitudes are further complications.

Highlights of my year in Germany:

1) 20 students per class or less (in 2000; now they are up to 30)
2) Interesting and varied class schedule
3) Plenty of time to prepare for classes in between classes
4) Exam schedule well planned in advance and scheduled so there was seldom more than one final per week during exam times.
5) Many social opportunities
6) Support from colleagues
7) Strong infrastructure designed to enhance the ability for students to learn and be taken care of when there is a social or academic problem
8) A multi-faceted school system with a multitude of options for students: Realschule (5-10 grades, trade-bound); Hauptshule (middle school); Gymnasium (college-bound high school); Gesamtschule (general high school); trade schools, adult schools, and apprenticeship programs (Berufsschule).

9) Regular grade conferences involving students, teachers, and parents in the evaluation of the student's progress
10) Specialized (Profil Classes) with designated field interest opportunities for students. This is much like School-to-Career or Career Pathways.

Personal Difficulties:

Being without a car because I lived quite a distance from my school with no regular bus schedule and a 15-minute walk with a heavy briefcase to the train station. I had to lug groceries on my back on a bike from town. That level of physical exertion was not the norm for me. I did purchase a used car and that solved a lot of problems.

Professional Difficulties:

Correcting the first set of finals was the most challenging thing I had to do. After I learned how to do it, it was no problem. Some conflict regarding my style of teaching became an issue for a while. There was quite a bit of discussion about how I should be teaching and that I must strictly adhere to their themes and procedures when I felt a new approach might be interesting for the students. I was compromising more by the second semester due to pressure from the department head and others. I often thought that it seemed kind of foolish to have a foreign teacher there if I couldn't do a few uniquely "me" things. I understood the need to prepare them for Abitur (finals), so I could see their point. However, there is something to be said for teaching them things that are not always lock-step. That's called critical thinking.

I haven't had an opportunity to talk to anyone but my local Toastmasters group about my experiences, but that is really sad because I went there to share these experiences with others, yet no one has the time to listen to me, so I write this book.

It is remarkable how different the systems are. Some of the things that I notice the most are: paperwork, maturity levels, state mandates, class sizes, and homework issues.

Every day we receive about 5-10 documents in the mail in our American schools. They are workshop information, conference details, grant possibilities, homework to be given to the absentees, notice of adds and drops, notices of parent/teacher conferences, confidential information about kids, attendance, tardy, truancy and sickness documentation for your own students, transfers of grades, final grades for withdrawals, notices from the credit union, daily bulletins, contest and exam dates and information, counseling calendars, surveys requested by colleges and state organizations, another list of all absences in the school, just to name a few.

Maturity levels of our students are about two years behind the Germans. Reason: we baby the kids way too much. I find myself nagging the kids about the most mundane things connected with doing their homework. It is understandable with the ninth grade; they do not differ much from the ninth graders in Germany. We give out binder dividers to all ninth and tenth graders to help them get organized, along with numerous instruction sheets and blank assignment sheets. Kids appear to be overwhelmed with the amount of work they have to do. They are taking six courses each year for the entire year and meet five hours a week as opposed to the Germans who take 12 courses a year (in the 12th and 13th grades) for three hours a week in each course. However, it is true that American students have a lot of extracurricular activities that occupy much of their time.

German students have optional interscholastic sports, or have private teams outside of school; and Americans predominately attend band rehearsals, club meetings, homecoming events or go to football, basketball, soccer, baseball, water polo, or about a dozen other sports events most weekends.

American students are basically totally dissatisfied with their studies unless they are college bound. The troublemakers are bigger trouble because they are not interested in what is happening in the classroom. It is like pulling teeth to get them on track. Their behavior usually results in being kicked out of class and when they come back, they are not connected to what is happening in class because they have been gone too long, or they plan to get the credit from a summer school class.

In Germany, however, if a student fails to pass on to the next grade, they have two possibilities: 1) repeat the school year during holidays or on a private basis. Then, they are tested with a written and oral exam on the first and second days of the new school year. If they receive a "sufficient" grade, they pass on to the next grade. 2) If they fail, they have to repeat the whole last school year. If a student is allowed to try a summer school class privately, it depends on his number of failures and/or overall grade point average. Allowable failures are for 2 subjects only, or their overall average cannot be more than a "C" to qualify them for extra help. As you can see, there is more attention paid to who qualifies for extra help and a standard testing measure to assure they are ready to move on. In America, there are not as many rigid standards until the state moves in with their mandates.

One year, at one of our first faculty meetings, we were informed that the state was mandating that students pass state exams and if they did not pass them in one year, they would send in state reps to intercede. If another year went by without improvement, they would threaten to fire half the faculty and replace the principal. With these threats looming over us, it makes it difficult to teach while students still have the same bad habits of laziness and lack of concern. I attempt to cajole them with patient questioning as to why they refuse to do the work. I threaten, I plead, and I demand, but nothing works. They simply have their own little minds made up that they will not do the work. I think that they have been complacent too long and no longer think that it is necessary to do much of anything and our nagging, both as teachers and parents, is just a dull droning sound in the distance. I think we must fail students for a couple of years, flooding the summer sessions with the delinquent kids making up courses. In some ways, I see it as a two-fold problem: on one side the parents may not mind if their kid attends summer school because they have a babysitter for half the day; on the other hand, the student knows summer school is much easier so they don't care if they flunk or not. However, we also have a flurry of summer classes being taken by the advanced kids, who are raking up credits so they have more time to do extracurricular activities during the regular school year and start to take college courses while still attending their last year in high school.

Homework is given in a fair way, offering many participation points for motivation and the only reason some students pass is because of the participation point system to encourage them to speak in class. Since the oral part of their education gets little attention in general, I feel it is justified.

We visited a couple of other schools, but my concentration was much more on my own school. I was more interested in the Gesamtschule structure because it was the closest thing to our schools here.

ADVANCED PLACEMENT
RIDING HIGH

GATE-These classes start in the first grade and the same kids stay together all 12 years. This creates an elitist atmosphere and the students are acutely aware of how they are different (superior). Most of these kids are upper middle class whites. Invariably, their parents are highly educated and in such fields as medicine, law, and engineering. They have extremely high expectations for their kids and their kids receive a top quality education. As I said before, in my area, they represent about 2-4% of the local population. Some of these students fall out of this category when they start high school (for whatever reason) so their parents are adamant about having the generalized classes be rigorous, as well. However, this is an impossibility for several different reasons: 1) class size (upwards of 45 per class can be the case); 2) vastly different reading levels; and 3) different economic/cultural backgrounds (some parents don't speak English and cannot help their kids with their homework). However, despite this fact, these upper middle class parents are the ones who run the school. They know the system and politics and can influence decisions being made in the district. And so they do. Their intention is meant well. Of course, they want a top quality local high school so they don't have to dole out the money for a private school. And they do what is the most logical thing to do in terms of the betterment of their child and their pocketbook: they sign them up for a favored sport or put them in the music program and see to it that they are there early or late (as the case may be) all through their formative years and high school. At the same time, they make sure that they remain on the Dean's List and encourage them to take extra hard courses to get those extra grade points. And nudge them into school politics. Run for office, they say, I'll pay for the ad campaign. Why do this? It looks good on their resume. It wins scholarships. And not just puny ones either. Some kids get the whole enchilada—four years at a prestigious university and not one dime expended by their well-to-do parents.

Now, I know that it sounds like I am criticizing these parents for doing an extremely smart thing. But where does that leave the rest of the parents? Literally in the dust as they see the golden boys and girls race away in their father's used Mercedes to Harvard and Yale.

We need a system that represents the entire population of kids. Not all kids (even upper middle class kids) want to go the route of ivy league. It is usually their parents who want that anyway. You know that's true. Here's a typical conversation between two upper middle class moms:

"So where is your son going to college next year?"

"Well, he has been accepted at UCLA, Berkeley, and Stanford. He simply can't make up his mind where to go and what he wants to do. Right now, he is finishing up the interior of a new rec room in our home." What about your daughter?"

"Oh, she graduated salutatorian and was offered a full scholarship to Yale. She thinks she wants to go into law."

"Thinks she wants to go, you mean she might not accept the scholarship?"

"Oh, she'll accept it alright or I'll sell her horses and put her in a private school in Switzerland." Unfortunately, the last thing they would ever admit is that their son or daughter is unhappy with the path they chose for them. If the parent graduated from university and their son or daughter does not want to go to college, it appears to reflect on them. That is, however, the parents' problem and should not be imposed on the kid. Once again, an attitude.

AGRICULTURAL PROGRAM
SURF'S UP!

A good example of rigor and excellence and meaningful pursuit of a specific career, you need only look at the agricultural program. In every aspect of that program, the student is held accountable and respected for their contributions. When they leave school after having been in that program, they have a complete understanding of their field of endeavor. They have employable skills. No one would ever suggest that agricultural students were not highly skilled and they are even revered as a body of people. They have had four years of practical applications of solid, work-related skills. Their outstanding club, Future Farmers of America, is the biggest club on campus at our school and celebrates their accomplishments every year by having a huge banquet inviting hundreds of people from the community, in which students are honored for their work. They are also taught numerous leadership skills to carry into life and their future interactions with others. If you want to see relevance in education, you need look no further than the ag department.

Our agricultural program is one of the most phenomenal programs that exist in our schools and its design and operation should be copied across the states. It offers a multitude of programs along the agricultural line, such as: horse care and judging, involving evaluation of horse performance & conformation, with an oral component to be judged at fairs. A small engines team that will troubleshoot engines that do not run, study engine theory, identify tool and engine parts, and problem solve any difficulties. A power mechanics team who will troubleshoot large engines and equipment, operate large equipment, and identify tool and engine parts. A welding/mechanics team, which is involved in arc welding, woodworking, electrical wiring, plumbing, tool identification, surveying, cold metal work, and electrical motors. There is a specialty animal team that identifies breeds of rabbits, dogs, cats, goats, guinea pigs, hamsters and rats. They also identify veterinarian/grooming equipment. Showing livestock at fairs is another major part of the ag program. They take beef & dairy cattle, sheep, hogs, horses, rabbits, and poultry to local fairs to be judged. Some of the courses offered at school are: ag science, animal science, dairy husbandry, ag mechanics, crop production, ROP ag leadership, advanced ag leadership, horticulture, agribusiness management, small gas engines, advanced small engines, intro to welding, welding technology, advanced equipment construction & principles of technology, which is designed to offer an introduction to all of the former classes. I have worked next to these ag teachers and I find them to be some of the best teachers that we have. The students are very focused on the program and their entire studies center around those activities. The students are generally highly motivated and excel in most of their ag classes. They have a definite goal and spend the entire four years geared toward that goal. At the end of an agriculture major, the following jobs are attainable: in animal science: technician in artificial insemination, animal health, vet assistant, animal nutrition, herd management, or biotechnology. Careers could result in becoming a vet, animal nutritionist, business owner, general manager, geneticist, game warden, biologist, environmental specialist, or ag teacher. In agribusiness management, jobs would be realtor, sales rep, inspector, office clerk, receptionist, bookkeeper, retail clerk, data entry, lawyer, lobbyist, stock broker, journalist, accountant, advertising specialist, consultant, P.R. director, loan officer. Working with power equipment, they could become a technician in electrical, mechanical, diesel repair, small engine, equipment set-up, computer operation, or hydraulics. In metal fabrication, possible jobs are shop foreman, contractor, technician as millwright, certified welder, blue print interpreter, computer draftsman, engineer, contractor, supervisor, CEO, or service trainer. As you can see, the possibilities are endless.

APPRENTICESHIPS
A TRICKLING STREAM
TO THE MIGHTY OCEAN

My husband was a product of the apprenticeship program (Berufsschule) as a young man growing up in Germany. He was put into a middle school up to 10th grade for his preliminary education. At 15, he went to work for a local fabricating business working in metal construction. He was paid a small amount of money per month for pocket money, which went up each year for the 3 and one half years he was apprenticed to this company. He worked four days a week doing the regular job training and one day was spent at a technical school where he spent eight hours doing the academic side of his training. As his final, he had 16 hours to complete a project designated by his instructor, spent four hours in orals and several hours in a written exam. At the end of the program, he was certified as a fabricator & machinist, employable by the company at a regular salary. This would be equivalent to a journeyman in the States.

This type of education serves several purposes both for the student and the business. The student is working hands-on in a field of his <u>choice</u>. As I mentioned before, in the 9th grade of a generalized high school (Gesamtshule) students are sent out for three weeks at the start of the school year and three weeks at the end of the school year to explore a field of their choice like: cooking, baking, electrical, mechanical, or clerking of some kind, just to name a few. Each student seeks his or her own place of work. They are not paid, but rather use it as a source of information to see if they like that type of work. This is the preliminary groundwork laid for them before their sophomore year in case they wish to segue into the program as early as the start of sophomore year. Others, due to desire or maturity level may wait to take such a position at the start of their junior year. At any rate, it serves the purpose for kids who are not interested in the traditional college-bound curriculum. You get them started in a field of their ability and interest and catch them before they lose interest in school. On the side of the business, they are training future employers to their standards and can expect to employ them at the end of the training.

We need to institute such programs. Instead of government funds being used for esoteric, fleeting, spur-of-the-moment programs that end up in the toilet after the funds expire, the government should be supporting local businesses to establish apprenticeship programs. Both parties benefit greatly and we lower the dropout rate considerably.

Some examples of how this works was experienced in my 9th grade class. One of my boys, a tall, more mature street-wise type kid went to cook for a restaurant at the start of his 9th grade year. They liked him so much that they invited him into their apprenticeship program as soon as he was finished with the 9th grade. He will be well paid and employed by the time he is 18, fully trained and certified in the art of cooking.

Another example was my physical therapist. She wanted to go to the trade school in the 5th grade, because she didn't want to work that hard. She was done at 16, and began working at an old folks home where she lived, as well, and was paid a small stipend. After her commitment was fulfilled, she was older and more mature and decided she wanted to do physical therapy. She then went to a tech school for two years and then was employed as a physical therapist in a retirement home. She was happy with her education and got through school with her interest still in tact. Supporting such programs will keep more students in school and off the streets, employable at an early age where they can become totally self-sufficient at 18. Presently, our kids have only a high school diploma which everyone knows is next to meaningless, and those kids who do not go on to college, end up in an indecisive, lax state before they decide to go to work.

BLOCK SCHEDULING
TIDE'S OUT

In American schools, the schedules vary considerably from town to town, city to city, and state to state. However, there is a traditional schedule that many schools still maintain. That schedule is comprised of 6-8 hours of school a day. Teachers get one prep period and teach five hours. Many schools have an early period for special classes or music programs and sometimes an eighth period for the same reason. Some schools may be on a year-round schedule, but generally it is for the lower grades. The schedule is the same everyday unless they have chosen a block schedule, which allows certain classes to be taught for a 90 minute period on certain days.

In a normal day, the teacher will see each of their classes every day of the week for about a 45-55 minute period. They are always the same period and the same students. Class sizes vary according to the school population. Class sizes can be as small as 10 or as many as 45. Depending on the district policy, there may or may not be limits on the class sizes. Most teachers have their own rooms. Depending on how crowded the school is you may or may not have to share a period or two with another teacher. Sometimes, teachers have to teach at two different sites.

In Germany, the daily schedule is totally different every day. There are no set prep periods because classes are at different times of the day and week. You meet with each class for one 45 minute period and one 90 minute period. It is never on the same day or in the same room. It could meet in the same room twice that week but not necessarily. Teachers must walk to a different class each period and do not have their own rooms. However, in this manner, you save the number of people moving about the school. It is much simpler to have 50 teachers moving, as opposed to 500 students.

My schedule was as such:

Mondays
Periods 1 & 2 Drama
Periods 5&6 Drama
Period 7 English 11

Tuesdays
Period 2 English 9
Periods 3&4 English 12
Periods 5&6 English 12
Period 7 English 11

Wednesdays
Early Period (7:05 am) English 12
Period 3&4 English for Chemistry Majors
Period 5 English 9

Thursdays
Period 3&4 English 11

Fridays
Period 1 English 12
Period 3 English 9
Period 5&6 English 11
Period 7 English for Chemistry Majors

As you can see, some days are incredibly full and other days, there is far more free time. I rather like the German plan simply because it offers a change in the schedule. It is more interesting, but on the other hand, the consistency of the American schedule is simpler to follow and you are always in your own classroom with your own set of files and books and materials.

In the German system you must always lug things around with you, and race from one end of the school to the other and up and down stairs. I was lucky enough to find a cubby hole (which I shared with a few other teachers in the map room) so I didn't have to keep all my materials with me all the time. However, when I wanted to check my mail or Xerox off materials, I had to go to another building and up the stairs. Teachers in Germany normally have a huge staff room in easy reach, two long breaks of 20-25 minutes between periods two and three and four and five. If there are separate buildings, there is always a staff room in each building, but not always with the same equipment.

This issue of having shorter versus longer has been such a controversial one at our school, although many schools have employed it and maintain that schedule or dropped it and gone back to the old traditional one. I think it is greatly beneficial to have a larger block of time with students to work on projects. A short period doesn't allow you to even get started on a project without a bit more time than what we have in a 48-52 minute period. Think about it. In a normal period, you have kids trailing in on time and about 1 or 2 who are regularly late. In the first period class this year, I had 4-8 kids late everyday. So, I lost five minutes of time just running over to my attendance records and scantrons to set the records straight. Attendance alone would cost at least 2-4 minutes depending on who just slipped out the door to go to the bathroom while taking attendance. I figure each day, given the other small chores that need to be done, like passing out paper and collecting homework, I probably have 40 minutes of actual instruction time. That just isn't enough time to thoroughly cover material.

In Germany, we met with students two times a week. One time for 45 minutes and one time for 90 minutes. It is quite common to teach main subjects like English and German, (but not math) in two 45 minute periods and one 90 minute periods from the 5th grade on. The purpose is to get the younger students used to concentrating for longer intervals and focusing on more complicated topics and longer texts. The biggest complaint in American schools is that very problem, lack of attention span for the less mature kids. Also, teachers complain they can never fill up that time with enough to do. All they have to do is provide two-day lessons for the double period.

In America, we have, for the most part, maintained the traditional schedule of six short periods a day, and I think it is time for a change.

BUSINESSES
TIDE'S IN

Local businesses need to make a contribution. They need to send representatives from several different businesses in town. A wide selection of businesses representing all levels of learning must be utilized. These business people must be invited to the meetings on a regular basis and there needs to be a school rep who coordinates all this. There must be a school person who handles setting up appointments and a general liaison between business leaders and the school. In every aspect of development of programs, there needs to be input from all people involved. In some junior high schools, business partnerships are already in place. Those partnerships need to be continued in high school.

In Germany, students in the ninth grade (and eleventh grade at Gymnasium, have two three-week practical training experiences during their freshman & junior year. This gives them the opportunity to explore a field in which they may develop interest later. I propose the same set-up once a semester. Companies gain free labor and kids gain free access to job opportunities. At the appropriate time, students can decide which field they choose to pursue and then transfer to a trade school. When building new schools, it should be a trade school that is built. In New Hampshire, they have a trade school that services the local high schools by bussing juniors and seniors over in the afternoon. I advocate total immersion the last two years in a trade school environment. Thereafter, they should earn a certificate of training that will make them employable locally. Part of the program should be part-time work at the work site of choice whereby they have a segue into the business as future job placement.

The concentration in the regular high school should be all college bound students in intensive courses like we now have, except the recipients will be students who are comfortable being there and have chosen that program free of will.

BEMOCRACY = THE RIGHT TO BE

HIGH TIME, HIGH TIDE

If we need to speak of a democratic system, then why isn't free will part of that equation? Students should have the right to choose what they want to pursue for their life's work. However, we must give them the opportunity to see what choices they have. Right now, the choices are too limited, and too limited simply because we are not properly informing them, motivating them, and encouraging them to build on their strengths.

I have never met a stupid child. Every single one has a gift. A gift from God, a strength that needs to be developed. If we assign them a rigid schedule of a pre-determined curriculum that does not in the least uplift that child's talents and self-worth, then it is useless. Yet, that is what I am seeing time and time again. They grow to hate school, authority, structure, and endless rules that serve to limit, not broaden that child's horizons.

There must be rigor in any course pursued, but apply the rigor in a curriculum for students with more options, thereby assuring their desire to learn if taught subjects relevant to their abilities, interests, and gifts.

A plan leading in this direction can start with federal funding given to businesses to encourage them to participate in concrete apprenticeship programs. Along with that, the local or neighboring junior colleges need to coordinate classes with the high school.

CAREER PATHWAYS
APPROACHING THE SANDY SHORES OF LIFE

The Career Pathways Program in Germany was comprised of several areas of interest. These were: 1) Corporation: Beautiful and Tasty; 2) Corporation: Good & Practical; 3) People & Nature; 4) Political Workshop; 5) Sports; 6) Fine Arts; 7) Media Studio; 8) Theatre; 9) Future Workshop; and 10) World in Touch. These pathways were offered to the ninth graders as part of a two year commitment. This gave students a focus in any area of their choice. At this time, they would switch homeroom teachers. This concerned a number of the faculty because they were accustomed to being with the same kids from 5th to the 10th grade. This continuity constituted a vast difference in the way the kids felt about their education, but they were willing to try this new idea. Here is a synopsis of the programs offered.

Corporation: Beautiful & Tasty

Today I finally made it to the Bistro. This is a class that runs a little bistro in one of the classrooms. The students painted and decorated a room with tables and chairs and coat racks and candles, a bar for soft drinks and a kitchen next door. Each Wednesday, they cook a meal and invite the teachers. It is rather expensive, but you get a main dish, dessert, coffee, and a soft drink for about 6 Euro ($7.50) with tip included. The students cook and serve and it was really a great idea. This is part of a multi-tiered career pathway called, "Corporation: Beautiful & Tasty". In their original curriculum plan they set it up as such: Year 1: a room in school was converted and used as a restaurant, fully equipped as a business, and decorated to resemble a restaurant. Preparation: brainstorm ideas for bistro; look for building materials, calculate costs, look for sponsors, divide up work. Prepare walls, tables, glassware, utensils, curtains, and lighting. Year 2: Run a restaurant, which is open to faculty & staff once a week, cook a meal, serve it, and collect income from tips. Their goals were: to prepare tasty, healthy meals, prepare a menu that is attractive. Organize by looking for recipes, calculate prices, and keep a budget. Maintain an attractive environment and learn how to serve customers in a timely, friendly, professional manner.

I believe this was successfully done, given that it was open each Wednesday and many faculty and staff members had their lunch there. I attended regularly after finding out it was there. They spent Tuesday shopping and preparing the menus and meals were cooked on Wednesday, and different students were able to serve to learn the trade. Then Thursday and Friday, they planned for the following week. This was a great way for kids to learn the restaurant business.

Corporation: Good & Practical

Students would establish a corporation and run it successfully by producing something useful for the students and community. Students must decide on the product and then advertise, purchase materials, and keep financial records. Work was divided up evenly with each person doing a different job from one year to the next. Products can be made of wood, metal, or textiles. Work can be done in groups or individually. Advertisement must be developed for each product. An entirely new project can be created. Product development must be of the highest standards. They worked with business people to procure the best prices on materials. They had to be willing to take on leadership roles in the business. They kept a budget, established goals and a solid work plan. A number of the products were on sale in the faculty room intermittently and were displayed and sold at our annual school fair.

People & Nature

The objectives are: 1) to take care of & observe animals & plants. 2) Ask & answer questions about natural science, biology, & chemistry. 3) Have a desire to change things and create awareness. 4) Have input into environmental questions & answers. 5) Develop own ideas and present evidence.

Actual activities: 1) Create a workroom/area in preparation of activities. 2) Keep the campus orderly and clean. 3) Repair and repaint when needed. 4) Keep hallways and pathways clear and clean. 5) Repair fences. 6) Keep classrooms in order. 7) Investigate the water & food sources. 8) Study the effects on soil. 9) Visit farms. 10) Create their own plant and food gardens for planting, harvesting, and study. 11) Conduct research on the lakes and streams around the community. 12) Conduct experimental testing of the water supply through microscopic studies of the water, animals, & plants. 13) Examine recycling issues and create a composting area. 14) Set up recycling bins around school and collect on a regular basis. This was all done at the school.

Political Workshop

Suggested themes: 1) Youth during the 50's. 2) Research on a political travesty. 3) Governmental politics. 4) Create your own topic. Examples: 1) Youth during the 50's: What was it like? 2) What was the situation after the war & the post-war situation? Was there peace in Germany, and a better standard of living? More security? Businesses thriving? 3) What was the your parents' childhood like? 4) Introduction of TV, black/white/1 program. 5) Introduction of the 5-day week. 6) Atom bomb experiments. 7) Rock 'n roll time period. 8) Love & sex in the 50's. The information could be obtained from interviews with grandparents/parents, library, archives, other people, museums, finding objects in attics or cellars. Have a party at school celebrating that time period.

Objectives: explore the past, watch daily news, consider being a politician, go on field trips to meet & talk with people, and to share your experiences with others in a concrete presentation.

Another idea: Research local political happenings. Like the Japanese internment or the Indian take-over's, or the history of the Hispanics in California. Of course, in Germany, the suggestions pertained to their areas of historical/political interests. An entire project could involve excavating, interviews, visiting museums, putting together a project for display or taking people on tours.

Other possibilities: Elections, where candidates are thoroughly examined and issues are studied. A live debate in school with critical issues discussed by all parties involved. Candidates should be invited, ads made for the event, flyers, and posters. All must be prepared ahead, deciding on issues, preparing questions, having question/answer period, and agendas written and posted, with follow-up correspondence.

Sports

Training to improve performance. Presentations & organizing of events. Twice a year, present a school-wide sporting event. Report on sports stories, learn about other types of sports, and train others.

Fine Arts

Organize a school-wide art display of student, parent, and professional work from the local area. Part of it can also be for sale. Talk to artists and convince them to participate, build picture frames, learn about the life of artists, describe and interpret artwork, work on advertising, build new display racks; repair older ones, work on special artwork for the presentation, write own biographies, learn different art techniques, and visit art shows.

Media Studio

Produce radio & TV shows, video clips, films, & radio programs, theme-based slides & audio shows, create a documentary, organize live school shows, and work with theatre groups to produce a film, produce a talk show or video production. Art class can be taken in conjunction with this.

Theatre

Year 1: Preparing theatre pieces. Year 2: Presenting show. Three parts are involved: 1) Acting 2) Costumes, props, technical aspects, and ads 3) Music. Goals: 1) Read scripts to decide on one play 2) Edit the play 3) Learn roles & practice 4) Build props, create masks, sew costumes 5) Decide on music and produce it 6) Make ads and develop programs.

Students must have a desire to: 1) Act, play an instrument, do technical work or general work backstage 2) Go to other theatre productions and learn about backstage operations 3) Learn all parts of production both on and backstage 4) Enjoy being before the public

Future Workshop: Experimenting, Building, Presenting

Students must have: 1) Concern for saving energy at school and observing the results of solar energy used by the solar roof at the school 2) Concern for water usage & build a water use system 3) Create a weather station & study climactic changes, collect data, investigate, & exchange world-wide information.

4) Research a theme of choice regarding environment and take part in a student competition. Students must be interested in: 1) Thinking about environmental problems and what you can do to solve it. 2) Work on daily projects that require regular and exact investigation & trying new experiments 3) Preparing presentations based on the investigations in a tasteful and interesting way 4) Work as a team.

What will be learned: 1) How one can use new energy & what problems are involved. 2) What energy possibilities there are and how they can be utilized at home & at school. 3) Whether climate changes are occurring and how it affects us. 4) How to collect weather data & how it can be utilized. 5) How to save water and how it can be used. 5) How modern information technology can be put to good use.

World in Touch

This pathway gives students the opportunity to be in touch with students elsewhere in the world. Students will be: 1) Establishing a school site in other countries. 2) Set up email correspondence with foreign students. 3) Do joint projects with others to collect data and publish information on differences in their school system, economics, politics, social structures, etc. 4) Plan fall school field trip for a week. 5) Coordinate schedules and make plans to meet. 6) Plan longer stays with host families and tours of foreign schools. 7) Keep logs of correspondence, activities and plans. 8) Stay in close contact with students to establish good relations and maintain an understanding of different lifestyles and social systems.

COUNSELORS
A LIFE PRESERVER?

In Germany, there are no counselors. Homeroom teachers replace counselors, (at least in the school where I taught). These homeroom teachers are in charge of the same kids for at least one to two years and in some schools, it may be every year, where the numbers are one to 20. In American schools, it is one to 600. Is there any wonder that we lose touch with the kids that slip through the cracks as they become mere numbers to the counselors until our little suicidal kids show up on the screen. Our counselors are drowning in paperwork and unheard of counselor/pupil ratios. Only a tidal wave of ineptitude can result. No wonder we have Columbines!

Along with a homeroom teacher, who also serves as a tutor, a social worker also helps kids. These two people handle all the problems that come up when there is an issue with a student. I find that the system works quite well. Also, the department head can be called in when things get really rough. For example, I came into class one day and the ninth graders had piled all the chairs in a heap and it looked like some were broken. As I was walking to class I heard all this commotion and I had a feeling it was my class because they were an exceptionally rowdy bunch. So, I wrote to the homeroom teacher of these kids and reported the kids that did it. I also informed the department head. As it turned out, the department head came to class one day to discuss the situation and clarify what would happen.

In California schools, the counselors are in charge of dealing with light-weight behavioral problems, like boyfriend/girlfriend issues, fights, parental problems, academic problems, teacher/ student problems, and other minor scrapes and bruises that come about in the course of a normal school day. Besides advising in that capacity, they also arrange their class schedules and rearrange them when complications arise. They also work with administrators and other faculty and staff as a team effort to deal with individual students who have special needs. For example, special ed kids have regular meetings where they meet with parents and discuss the student's progress. For more serious problems, students are referred to a newly acquired "crisis intervention counselor" when the situation gets too sticky. Case in point. I had a student who had a sleep deprivation disorder and hadn't slept a solid night for five years. He came to school, needless to say, quite cranky, and got on everyone's nerves. He would make rude racial remarks, at random, to other students not of his race, and enflame even the most docile student with his remarks and his deprecating attitude. He often had headaches and couldn't focus on anything in class, so that led to misbehavior because he felt so lousy and didn't care about anyone or anything. Imagine not getting a full night's sleep for five years! The situation got so bad that he was getting into fights all the time, and even the nicest kids hated him. Well, three quarters of the year went by before any of his teachers knew about this. We only knew that he was difficult and seldom did any homework and was greatly disliked by his fellow classmates. A meeting was finally called with all his teachers and the crisis counselor. That is when the whole story emerged. According to the crisis counselor, this young man was so sick of feeling lousy all the time, having excruciating headaches and never fitting in, that he told her he was prepared to commit suicide. An added wrinkle was that his dad had died when he was one, and he felt like his dad was trying to contact him, so dying seemed a reasonable alternative. Add to that, being caught with a girly magazine in the classroom and finding out that his younger sister was also not sleeping at night, we began to conclude that this young man was, indeed, quite troubled. Then we found out that his mother, who only spoke her native tongue, could not communicate with her son because he refused to speak to her. Therefore, we concluded that this young man was a likely candidate for violence since he wanted to commit suicide anyway and was deeply alienated from other students because of his hostile behavior. Another situation was as follows: a young lady (age 16) came into class one morning. I could tell she was upset, so I called her out of the room and asked her if she was upset about something. She threw herself in my arms and began to cry. It turns out, the day before at 6:30 am (before school started) she was raped by a neighbor who grabbed her on the way to the store in an empty lot across the street from the school. She was beside herself. I asked to have another teacher take over my class and I walked her down to the counselor. Fortunately, the crisis counselor was coming in that day and we only had a short wait. I consoled her as much as I could until the professional arrived, explained what I knew and then rushed back to class.

Along with gang-related activities of all kinds, like weapons on campus, drive-by shootings, drug dealing, and a myriad of other activities practiced by 51 gangs in our rural town, we are also dealing with rapes, depression, suicides, and the list goes on.

This is just some of many such examples that must be referred beyond the normal counselor. To top all this off, each counselor is handling a workload of over 600 kids! Imagine that. We only have one counselor per grade level, and our school services 2400 students!

CONFERENCES
BOTH BUOYS & GIRLS BENEFIT

Conferences in California schools are almost always the result of crises. It starts out with a counselor/student, then counselor/teacher, then counselor/parent/teacher, then counselor/student/ parent/teacher, and then an all-out all teacher conference with either parent, other administrators and/or Special Forces to deal with the particular crisis at hand.

In Germany, conferences occur regularly several times a year and every single student is accounted for with parents, teachers, and other student advocates present. Grades are passed out to everyone so all students' grades are brought to the forefront. The homeroom teacher passes them out for their kids. Each student is then discussed in terms of their overall performance, noting any problems academically or personally. Feedback is given at that time from all twelve of the teachers who have that student.

Grades

Intercepting Stormy Weather

After all grades have been recorded, a copy of the grades are Xeroxed off and handed out to the teachers involved. There is a meeting held that starts out with one student and the parents. The student and parents are asked if they have heard about any problems. The student reports his perspective on the class and whether he has heard undue complaints from his peers. Then the parents are asked if their kids have reported anything at home that might be of concern. If there are no complaints, then the teachers talk about the dynamics of the class, and if there is any problems with certain kids in relationship to other kids. Normally, parents are only there if the student has an issue with a teacher or class.

Once we have ascertained there are no problems, the kid and the parents must leave and then the teachers talk among themselves about any problems. Now that meeting takes place twice a year. The second time includes looking at all the grades collectively. We then discuss any problems with kids and based on their cumulative average will be placed in a Realschule, Hauptschule, or Gymnasium. This was with the ninth graders, so there was a general consensus taken as to whether these kids should go on to a college bound school or trade school.

Teachers are torn as to whether there is enough time to discuss each child thoroughly, which in this case, a harried department head had several more of these meetings ahead of her and did not want to take a lot of time to discuss each case. It was a case of overload for her, and she should have had her conferences scheduled a little more apart.

Grade Conferences

Personal Account

Today was the last conferences with parents, students and teachers to discuss the collective grades of all students. To date, students who came were merely tokens and didn't say much or didn't come at all. However, two students from one of my classes attended the last session today with many complaints about their grades and how they were determined. They even mentioned specific courses and I was waiting to be lambasted, but they attacked earth science, physics, and math. They really were critical and each of those teachers had to justify the students' claim of either papers being returned late or no knowledge of what to expect from their grades. One teacher got very defensive and angry after being confronted. This, at last, was a real encounter between a student concern and the teacher response. Yesterday, we had a parent there who was complaining (for her child) about a grade. She really presented a vehement case for supporting her daughter in getting her grade revised. The teacher had to defend himself to the department head later.

On the positive side, it was a good opportunity to discuss any problematic students. At this time, you have a chance to hear about any students that are having problems, or say nice things about kids. Of course, we are looking at about 80 kids per level, so keeping track of that number is much better than 750, which is what we have.

The day before, I went to the tech high school, where my chemistry kids spend half their time and we had a conference with the teachers there. So half their time is spent in the tech high school and half the time in the regular one. The only problem with teaching English to these kids is that they all come from different schools and different levels of English so trying to discuss scientific articles with them when they can barely understand regular English is a bit of a challenge. About five speak and write English very well, and the others are all at vastly different levels, so I have resorted to teaching them general things. We read regular stories with regular dialog.

Another big difference in terms of dealing with kids is the class size. No classes in the upper levels are allowed to go over 20. That makes a big difference in terms of every aspect with which these kids are dealt. Also, the same teacher keeps track of these kids for that year and the safety net is vast when one teacher is in constant contact with what's happening with a student.

Parent Conferences

Once a year, right after the end of first semester, parents are allowed to make an appointment with a teacher to discuss their son or daughter's academic situation. An evening and one whole day is set aside. Each teacher is assigned a room and the parent shows up and is given a 20 minute session for discussion. It is a good opportunity to get to know parents and understand certain problems of kids. Now, in other school systems, in Germany, parents are allowed to come anytime to discuss their child's situation, and the teachers each have 1 hour a week dedicated to parent conferences. Otherwise, there are 1-2 days each semester dedicated to parent conferences; somewhat like the states, where we generally have 1 open house per semester but it is done collectively, rather than individually. Generally, the schedule does not allow for more than 15 minutes to address a class of parents and no time for a private conference about an individual child.

Highlights of my sessions in Germany:

The first mother was coming in to meet me and wasn't concerned with her daughter's grades because she was already doing well. She was extremely nervous and I could tell she had been drinking. She mentioned that she thought I gave too much homework the first semester.

The second session was regarding one of my special students who had a speech problem and major problems in English and German because of a brain defect. Both parents came in to see how I was handling him. I made it quite clear that I thought their son was quite gifted and a wonderful human being. They were not concerned about his grades as long as they knew he was putting out an effort and he always did. They were happy and I was happy to sing his praises.

One of my most puzzling and challenging students had his father pop in at the last moment. He was also a teacher and invited me to sit in on his classes and interview him for my book. He was fascinating and reminded me a lot of his son in his mannerisms. He was effusive about his appreciation of my teaching them summaries since that is such a big hot deal here.

One mother came in and discussed her son and a bad experience with a math class. She actually cried about the fact that the math teacher had said something insulting about her son's lack of ability in math. She was also upset that her son was now turned off to finishing the traditional education and would terminate at the end of the eleventh grade to pursue an apprenticeship program.

One of my ninth grade parents came in for her son and he was with her. He is a solid B student and a little sweetie and we all agreed that he would be keeping up his grades. He will be going on to an apprenticeship program after the tenth grade in health care of the elderly or some other related field.

One of my mothers came in to discuss how her son was caught up in a death in the family and several other major crises for which he had gotten terribly behind. I was very sympathetic and we agreed that he would eventually get things made up. He is not a very good student, and I predict that he may have a tough time getting things taken care of. Time will tell.

The last session was with a very concerned father regarding his daughter and we ended up having an unusual conversation about the class that she is in, in particular. It seems that one of my eleventh grade classes is having a hard adjustment into the upper grades due to the fact that their homeroom was split up after many years together as one group and that was a major transition, along with a more rigorous program. I told him that I felt that classes were cancelled too often. I also have them at the end of the day on Monday and Friday, when we are all exhausted. Also, it just so happens that those days are often picked as short days for one reason or the other. Anyway, he was quite upset about the cancellations and wanted to take it up with the department head. I asked him not to because our department head will likely come after me for mentioning it. Anyway, I didn't know what he would do.

The culminating experience was when I got trapped between the back of my car and the stone wall in the teacher's parking lot. It had been snowing prior to leaving, so I started the motor, and went to the back window to get the snow off and the car started rolling. I was totally frozen and didn't know what to do as it descended upon my kneecaps with a thud. I panicked and started screaming, "Help! Help!" instead of Hilfe, and then I relaxed, took a deep breath and tried to hold the weight of the car off me while I whistled one long, shrill whistle. A couple rounded the corner and saw my dilemma and rushed to my assistance. No broken kneecaps (it would have looked like a gang-related injury) and come to find out, it was the parents of another one of my ninth graders. We had a nice chat about their lazy son, and I was on my way. Rescued in the nick of time before my kneecaps were totally destroyed.

COLLEGE PREP
A LIGHTHOUSE BEACON . . . BEAMING THE LIGHT ON SOME QUESTIONS

College prep classes, in America, are what is offered most to our students. It is an equality issue. No doors should be closed to any student. All students should have the equal opportunity to go to college. However, the quotient that is left out is that many of these kids are not interested in college. They want to do hands-on work. They are good at it, it is relevant to them, and they feel focused when doing something meaningful. However, that is not how the system works. We are going to fit that round kid into a square hole if it breaks the system to do it. Why are we battling the Goliath of indifference? For the sake of equality? Does it make sense to let kids drop through the cracks and eventually drop out of school completely because we insist on being politically correct? Where does the equality issue end so that we can let the quality issue begin?

Perhaps we need to ask the parents this question. Do you really fear that your child will be discriminated against if he/she learns a trade instead of going to college? Have you ever thought to ask your son/daughter what they would prefer to do? Have you never reflected on an astounding talent they might have that you have noticed the last several years that could translate into something other than a college degree? Do you feel ashamed of your son/daughter because they want to be a mechanic or hairdresser when you have a Ph.D.? Do you attach college degrees to self-worth? Do you feel you have failed as a parent if John or Jane wants to travel another educational route than the one you chose? Are you a minority afraid that your child will not have the same opportunities as the upper middle class Whites?

When do we include our children in on the decision-making? When do we begin to offer them more than college prep courses? Do we really think we are serving them to the best advantage in this manner? Think about it as you read the following excerpt:

UC Regents approved a new way to "benefit high-achieving students in low-performing schools and late academic bloomers ("UC" B4). This, of course, includes my school in California's Central Valley, known for the low income area and higher unemployment rates. It sounds like a great idea because it "grants simultaneous entry in a high school student's senior year to a designated community college and a UC campus" ("UC" B4). That is all well and good, but the following criteria has been imposed:

The program is open to students in the top 12.5 percent of their high school class who don't have the grades, test scores or courses to qualify as UC freshmen. It is expected to admit up to 3,500 students a year. ("UC" B4)

This may also exclude the top 4 % who are automatically guaranteed admission as freshmen into a UC with the right grades and courses. At any rate, these percentages tell the whole story.

We are talking about 16.5 percent of the total high school population who are covered for university and college. The eternal question remains: what about the other 83.5 %? Those are the kids we need to help.

According to a recent Internet report, college may be a complete turn-off for many students. Should a four-year college degree be the goal for every student in America? Maybe not, says a recent report by Harvard University.

The report, "Pathways to Prosperity," says the American education system places too much emphasis on attending and graduating from a four-year college, and should instead emphasize training for jobs that don't require a four-year degree.

Today on American Morning, T.J. Holmes asks Robert B. Schwartz, co-author, and academic dean, Harvard Graduate School of Education, his response to critics who say all students deserve the dream of going to college. Should the American education system change its focus so that all students can thrive? These are current questions that are being asked about our educational system. ("Pathways to Prosperity" Feb 4, 2011)

DAY WITH THE DANES

I went with a colleague of mine to Denmark for a week with 14 of our kids and we met other students, went to their school and had activities together while we were there. It was a wonderful opportunity to bond with others. Here are the details of our trip:

I spent the night before our school field trip to Denmark with friends and came back home to pack. Little did I realize that we would lug our baggage so far and change transportation so often. We boarded the s-bahn in Bergedorf, changed to the train in Hamburg. I had a backpack and two other small bags, which was way too much! After we got off the train, we transferred to the ferry, which entails a great deal of walking up and down stairs. We were on the ferry for one hour and then walked through many corridors and steps again to get out of the ferry terminal. From there, a few of us were allowed to ride in a taxi van where we loaded all the baggage. The rest of the kids and Astrid, my colleague, walked. When we arrived and checked in, we then had to lug all our baggage another four blocks to get to our chalets. Ugh! That was the pits! We settled in. The chalets were cute. Upstairs sleeping quarters like on a ship. Very crowded and claustrophobic. The first night there was no wind at all and the mosquitoes were out in force. They were the size of a fly and biting like a spider. So, I felt better to leave the window shut and be stifled all night than to wake up with bites all over my body. There was already evidence of slaughtered blood-filled mosquitoes squashed on the ceiling.

We spent the whole day swimming in the Ostsee (Baltic Sea). Two boys immediately plunged into the ocean, so I followed suit. It was a bit chilly, at first, but after awhile, the softly rolling waves were a gentle caress to the soul. We then rented bikes and rode for a mile along the dike by the ocean and then loped off into the countryside and circled back around. On the dike, we found a nude beach and plunged into the ocean together. Up to that point, Astrid did not go into the water. But, soon she was going in too. We ate at a fast food place, which was horrible. We then ate a light meal at home that night.

We got up early and proceeded over to the school. There, I interviewed a number of kids and got a look at their school system. It was refreshingly different. I talked to teachers and took notes. Some of the kids were especially receptive and nice. Some information about the Danish school system follows: all students call their teachers by their first names. Most all of the schools in Denmark have their grades set up together from grade 1-10. Everyone teaches the same program, but within the classroom itself, the teachers decide on how the subject is approached. For example, better students are given more to read. They take exams in the ninth grade. They can then decide to go to university-bound or tech school, by choice. If they decide to go to college-bound, the teachers must concur. They are only required to go to school until they are 15. If they don't pass ninth grade testing, they go another year. There are two levels of tests and students decide which to take. Students begin to learn English in the fourth grade. They are nine years old.

In terms of tech school, they must attend one full year and work three years at a business. They take classes for five weeks, and then work three or four months, then repeat the process. 50% of the students go to tech school. In the 10th grade only, students can choose to go to a business and work for one month in October and then again later in the year. They work there to see if they like it. That is similar to the German system. Some students go on to Gymnasium to prepare for the university. Another student I talked to is going into a special program for social work; another will go to a dental assistant school.

Students who cannot pass the tenth grade, are practically non-existent because they can decide for themselves to not take a test if they have some other idea of a job. If a student isn't doing well in the ninth grade, they are tutored to come up to par. One student came from a sports-oriented school for a year; and then to the regular school and she prefers to be back in the specialized school because she plays soccer. Another student wants to work with children, so she will go to a special school for this (preschool training).

After spending the day at the Danish school, we went swimming at the indoor paradise. It was quite interesting aside from the hectic ways to get into the pool area. Everything European always seems to be much more complex! Home to a meal of peppered smoked mackerel, which was great! Now to bed, to bed. Another day is about to dawn.

Ostsee Interlude at LaLandia

Little pointy houses line the Ostsee shore
Little tiny windows beckon you once more.

Gentle, lapping waters caress your body there
And once you're in the water, they float away your cares.

Long, winding pathways must be traversed each day
If you haven't got a bike to ride along the way.

Shopping places exist both here and there
And if you're brave enough, you'll swim in the ocean bare

A big ole' swimming paradise sits right there in the middle
And through the turnstile entrance, everyone has to wiggle.

Rocks and waterfalls and slides adorn the atmosphere
And once you've found your way there, you simply have to
cheer

Several nooks and crannies are built for kids to play
With hot tubs and lazy lagoons for adults along the way.

The wind blows music through the air
Unless, of course, a baby's cry is there

For kids and parents come here each and every year
It certainly is no doubt that vacation is spent here

Yet in the fading months of fall
You can't predict the weather at all

Wind and rain, clouds and sun
You're lucky if you have just one.

So, come aboard the ferry and don't forget to see
That all your cares and worries can be left for just a week.

SUZANNE ZURILGEN STRAUSS

Ein Ostsee Abendteuer

Ein Ostsee Abendteuer is hier zu geniessen
And everyone will sure to be apleasin'

Der Wind is kuehl und wunderbar
The leaves rustle and beckon from afar

Ich habe das Land in Daenemark so gern
I find something different at every turn.

Das Fahrrad ist wichtig hier zu haben
So that your feet will not be sobbin'

Schwimmen tut man gern in der See
Unless you simply wish to stay away

Du musst doch Mut haben nicht zu frieren
And when you come out, you feel like cheerin'

Die See kann wirklich kalt sein
If, for warmer weather, you pine

So, Du musst immer sehen wie kalt es ist
Because your body will be put to the test.

Bleib mutig und versuche immer stark zu sein
And please be sure to bring some wine!

DIFFERENCES IN THE SOCIAL WHIRLPOOL
(A HUMOROUS LOOK)

Getting groceries—

When you go to the grocery store, you better be Speedy Gonzales, and Petula Preparation because it is a race to the finish! First of all, you have to train yourself to remember to bring your own grocery bag because you will either have to pay for yet another plastic bag (you have a trillion at home already) or withstand a disdainful stare while the cashier hands you one. Then you have to start bagging as soon as the first fruit or vegetable hits the counter top after being rung up. You furiously bag, trying to think of how your bagboy at home did it. Heavy stuff on the bottom, light stuff on top. However, you forget that the cashier does not think in terms of heavy bottom because inevitably after you have bagged everything, there's the jar of mustard that must be placed on top of the tomatoes. Heaven forbid you ask for another sack. Then, when she announces the amount, you drop everything and fumble in your wallet for the right change. After that, she is already ringing up the next customer who is nudging me out of the way with their bags poised for packing! I am still trying to figure out how to lug these bags to my car since there is also no one to help you with that. You then add that plastic bag to the dozens you have in your back seat and off you go to home.

The Naked Truth: Exploring a German Leisure Spa

The naked truth is that we Americans are quite puritanical. Now, I understand why it is, given our history. After all, Europeans escaping religious persecution settled our country. And now I think I understand what decadence they were trying to escape, after my visit to one of Germany's leisure spas.

It all started with a Fulbright Teacher Exchange Program for a year in Germany. Of course, I wanted to learn of all the cultural differences so I accepted an invitation to the sauna with some of my new friends. I packed my usual gear, swimsuit and towel, and headed for my German friend's house on a snowy evening. When I transferred to her car, she nonchalantly asked if I had ever been to a European spa. I said I had and I knew they indulged in co-ed nudity. So, all matters taken care of, we arrived at 9 pm on a Saturday night. Even she wasn't prepared for the crowd we encountered. Nowhere could we find a parking space in the enormous parking lot.

After changing clothes in the locker room, I was handed a bathrobe and we headed out for the biggest surprise of my life. A crowd of robed and disrobed men and women were jiggling, I mean jockeying for positions in the hallway, waiting for the shower or a spot in the sauna. It was a train station atmosphere with a twist . . . everyone was buck-naked!

I was instructed to take off my robe and shower . . . along with twenty other men and women crowding around the eight showerheads. Then we put our robes back on and paraded outside and through the dark, over wooden bridges and stone steps to a little wooden hut on the edge of the lake. There we entered a Finnish sauna with thirty other naked men and women. The room was dimly lit, so there was no need to "sweat" the small stuff. So what if your tummy had erupted into a six-month pregnancy. Who was looking? Well, I did the California thing when sequestered in a party-like setting, I suggested we sing. Several people chuckled and then I sang the first few bars of a German song and that broke the ice and before you knew it, they all knew I was a California girl. I had established rapport.

Then, the spa trainer came in to add scented water to the rocks. He then did a dance with the towel to spread the heat, and finally he handed out ice to cool our limbs (and libido).

After that, it was a potpourri of sauna settings. Open fire, smaller rooms, bigger rooms and in between a duck in the ice-cold pool or a hosing down by a friendly bystander.

Then, outdoors again to the lap pool for forty laps in the falling snow. (Here we actually needed to put on our suits.) That is until 11 pm when the regular swimmers went home and the die-hards stayed on in the whirlpool for candlelight and classical music and disrobing again.

Everyone floated and soaked and it seemed like the most natural thing in the world. And puritanical me . . . ? I loved it! But I couldn't help but think of the Romans in their bathhouses, and a little bit of wickedness as naked men and women's bodies glimmered in the candlelight! I guess my Christian psyche was shattered a bit because for several days afterward I felt guilty. When I e-mailed my pastor to ask if it was a sin to go to a co-ed sauna, he wrote back that it was a MORTAL SIN because men just didn't know how to behave themselves in front of naked women. Later, I asked a German priest what he thought and I was assured that as long as I went there with pure thoughts that I was not committing a sin. The naked truth is we're all the same, in the end, no matter what shape we're in, and I ended up writing a little poem to commemorate the event in my life . . . it's called:

Sauna Sins

I approached the sauna with great trepidation
Thirty naked bodies crammed, like in a station.
There was hardly room for anyone to sit
So I squeezed in between bare feet and a tit
There were body parts strewn left and right
And I knew in a minute I must look a fright
Then coyly I looked all around me just then
And noticed some fat ones, some plain ones, some slim.
It really didn't matter; we all looked the same
We weren't there to get fancy prizes and fame
We wanted to relax and be social too
Just hoping we wouldn't see someone we knew
Now Germany's known for its liberal exposures
While Americans are terrified of public disclosures
So the next time you want to visit a German spa
Make sure there's no one there you know at all

Driving in Germany

Roads in Germany were intended for horse and carriage not motor driven vehicles! What that means is that you have to learn patience and consideration when driving most streets in the city and its outskirts. I call it "kamikaze" driving because you never really know if the person heading for you will actually stop if a car is parked in their way. The protocol is that if you have a car or cars in your way, you must stop and let the oncoming car go first. Sometimes, both drivers make a snap judgment and go for the gold, narrowly missing each other while passing. Sometimes, another person does not adhere to the protocol and bombs ahead of you and nearly drives you off the road. Sometimes, if you are driving on automatic pilot, you simply pass without checking to see if there is someone coming. Then you must suffer that outraged look of disbelief or horror depending on how close we come to hitting each other. Buses also swerve in and out playing Russian roulette with the other cars. Roads are so narrow in the back roads that watching a truck approach, is tantamount to aborting your journey for the day and taking your chances in the nearest ditch. After you manage to survive that particular situation, a bus approaches quickly and you are just short of closing your eyes in an attempt to escape the inevitable possibility of rolling your car.

German driving also includes the eternal traffic jam, which occurs regularly for a variety of reasons. The biggest cause is road construction, but also includes, slow moving cumbersome farm equipment, weather conditions, and over-populated areas with thousands of people converging on the same general location. Making a left turn is taking your life into your own hands. They mark the area where you can wait, which lies with your front end just into the oncoming lane so that the cars behind you can pass while you wait to turn. Of course, out of fear, you may not have your front end on the line exactly, which means that the cars behind you are blaring their horns and the oncoming cars are swerving to avoid you. By this time, the light has turned red and you are still in the intersection waiting for a grand slam from some other car. To make matters worse, by the time you make the turn, some smart ass pedestrian is shaking his head at you like he has the last word on making turns in heavy traffic!

Then, I shall take you into the realm of parking your car in Germany. Or one could rephrase it by saying squeezing your car into a parking place. Number one, there is no way you can park in any crowded area without the magic key: visualization. When I set out for a specific place, I imagine the store in my head and I see a parking place very close to it. When I arrive, some car is just leaving. You just must be sure that you have positioned yourself to nab that sucker before some sneaky person beats you to it. Also, the automatic parking ticket machine is tricky. You can only pay for one half hour or one hour at a time. No more. So, guess what? You are constantly returning to the car, but guess what else? No one gives a hoot because there is no one there to check to see if your ticket is expired.

That brings us to the next point. Police. You never see them. I asked my cousin, who is a policeman himself why I never see policemen stopping people. He said there are cameras! Cameras!

That really made me paranoid. Supposedly (it hasn't happened to me yet) a light bulb goes off as you venture down the road at a forbidden speed. Then 4 weeks later, you receive a little notice in the mail with a picture of yourself white knuckling your way down the road. Oops! Caught. The only time you see the police is when their whaw whaw whaw sirens go off and you try to squeeze to the side of the road to avoid being slammed against everybody else you are trying to avoid.

EXCEPTIONAL KIDS
(EXCERPT FROM ARTICLE)

Another article in the local paper (Stanley <u>Monterey County Herald</u> May 28, 2000 F4) dealt with parents and their own anxiety over their kid's acceptance to certain "high-end" programs for the so-called "gifted" child. It stated that parents tend to work themselves into a tizzy if their child is not accepted to these programs. In fact, in one case a ". . . woman was considering legal action against a school . . ." because her son was not part of the gifted program. In our school, we call them AP's (for advanced placement). According to Dr. Stanley, (who wrote the article), he thought that this woman felt that the act of not being part of the AP population would label her son as a failure, as if only those students who are in that program will succeed. In our school those AP kids comprise 2-4%, so that means, (and this was Dr. Stanley's observation in the article), that only 20-40 kids out of a thousand have the chance of being truly successful. Of course, as I outlined in another chapter, these are the kids that rush off directly to university, so they can be done with graduate school at the ripe old age of 24. However, does that make them any more successful than the student who waits to finish his education at 28 or 30? Somehow, certain social groups deem it necessary to force their kids into their ideal mold and anything short of that, is less than acceptable. Furthermore, according to Dr. Stanley, the mother's belief system could truly influence the way her son feels about himself. If she believes that being outside the AP environment equates to failure, perhaps her son will also pick up on that and feel less adequate. Teenagers are notorious for fulfilling their parents' expectations of them. So, mom says, "You'll never amount to anything if you don't take those AP courses". Then the son ends up in other-than-AP and decides that since Mom already has predicted what will become of him, he might as well not disappoint her. He, therefore, fails to even pass mediocre classes. According to Dr. Stanley:

> ... Life is not one short race—it is a marathon of marathons. Labels come and go. If you believe that you can succeed in life in spite of degrading labels that predict your failure, you are likely to win most of the marathon. This is the common experience among millionaires. The large majority reports that at some point or points in their lives they were labeled inferior, average, or mediocre, but they did not allow critics to forecast their future achievements, and they overcame their label of so-called inferiority. (Stanley F4)

In surveying millionaires, Dr. Stanley found that many had an average G.P.A., and non-exceptional experiences in school, some did not even attend college, but their most noted remembrance was learning, somewhere along the way, something about the work ethic and the importance of hanging in there for the long haul. They also learned more from social interactions inside and outside school, as well as holding a part-time job on the side. These are attributes hard to identify with among many of our immediate-gratification-youth, where everything has to move as fast as the racecar they are driving in the video arcade. Where action has to be producing more action to keep them engaged. Very little comes from themselves because they feel the need to be entertained. Whereas, this summary of how millionaires viewed their education had a lot to do with social interactions where they were able to make accurate judgments about people. These social interactions are much more part of the American system via clubs and other extracurricular activities inherent in the school system here. There was also mention of developing a multitude of skills, such as all eight levels of intelligence. The more you strive for the Renaissance Man Syndrome, the more successful an individual can be.

It is more than studying a specific course in school or college, or high grades, rank, and SAT's. The really big influences have generic labels such as: strong work ethic, effective time or resource allocation, judgment, tenacity and empathy. (Stanley F4)

Dr. Stanley admonishes parents to not fall into the trap of a self-fulfilling prophecy that having their child not do well in school will condemn them to failure.

A personal case in point has to do with my own experience. I was a "C" student during high school in the upper track classes at the time. I cannot recall whether we had AP classes, but we did have A and B tracks. A was for college-bound; B for the rest. I was in A, but I could not compete with my upper middle class classmates whose parents were college-educated. My father didn't even finish the eighth grade and my mom took a couple of junior college classes for fun after she graduated from high school. I then went to Europe for 19 months and came back and went to junior college for three years. I barely passed my SAT's and had to take Bonehead English and Bonehead Math. I had a part-time job and took only 2-3 classes per semester to get my GPA up. My counselor even told me that with such low SAT's; I could not consider transferring to any substantial university. When I told him I wanted to go to UC Berkeley, he told me I could never handle it. I applied anyway and was accepted. I was there a year, transferred into a student exchange program in Germany, came back, finished at Berkeley with a BA and went on to get my masters in education at the University of New Hampshire. So much for discouragement. To this day, I am still a lousy test-taker and I de-emphasize it in my classes, because my focus is on identifying as many different levels of intelligence in my classes and helping them to apply not just test taking skills, but these other valued skills mentioned by Dr. Stanley. Personally, I believe in discipline, time management, organizational skills, social skills, and determination with a big dollop of enthusiasm and a positive attitude. These are the cornerstones of education for my kids and me in the classroom.

It boils down to much the same thing that Dr. Stanley espouses and recommends to the people with whom he interacts. Exceptional kids come in lots of different packages and they are not all labeled "AP"!

This school is still going strong and this is their philosophy:

Many young people do not thrive in large public schools, particularly if they are unusually creative, have non-traditional learning styles, and need to belong to a small supportive community of learners. We pay attention to the whole person: body, mind and spirit. In a small, supportive environment, personal characteristics that might be labeled a disability in a larger school become an appreciated diversity.

Our country is in great need of active, knowledgeable citizens. Young people need to learn to be members of the "commons" by being active citizens who are aware of social, political and environmental issues and know how to be pro-active in the public domain. The school is governed by an All School Meeting, made up of students, parents, educators and community people. Students govern day-to-day operations through a consensus decision making process. They have a lot of responsibility. Students do community service, work on referendums of their choice, join local organizations such as Seeds of Peace and will eventually serve on town boards. (Internet 2012)

FINALS
SMOOTH SAILING OR A ROCKY LANDING

Finals are taken very seriously in Germany. They are given twice a semester and they follow a specific essay format. That format is: comprehension (by writing a summary), analysis (by interpreting lines), and comment (by stating their opinion).

Correcting these essays is a monumental task. The papers must be folded so that one third of the paper is left free for corrections. That's where the corrections are written. You read through the papers to correct general errors and assign a content grade, which consists of structure and an understanding of text. A second reading is to catch the mistakes you missed the first time. Then you assign half points or whole points to the mistakes with an explanation (in abbreviation) next to it. After the notations are made with the points, you must count the points, divide by the number of words they wrote (they must count them themselves) which means trusting teenagers (?????) and then compare it to a chart which indicates a quotient that corresponds to a number that will be used as the grade for the number of mistakes made. The third grade is command of language which is a grade linked with the number of mistakes made. If too many mistakes are made, the command of language naturally drops.

These three grades are then averaged together and then the chart is once again perused to figure the number grade. Twelfth grade has a scale from 1-15; the eleventh grade from 1-6; so that means that you must look at two different charts.

While teaching at Gesamtshule Bergedorf, there were hefty discussions as to whether my methods were acceptable in writing up finals. The Germans contended that they must be completed precisely like their final year exams so the students would know exactly what to expect. That is why they established such rigorous standards regarding the grading of papers.

GETTING THE MOST
OUT OF SCHOOL
STUDENT ESSAY
BY BRIAN JOHNSON (2001 GRADUATE)

Learning how to invest properly is a very important thing that a person must learn in life to be truly financially successful. Investments will be a person's main source of income if that person is to be truly successful. It is said that very wealthy people make roughly 60-65 percent of their income through their investments. If investing is so important to life and becoming successful, why isn't it taught in school?

Historically, the school system has told students that working hard and getting good grades will almost guarantee future success in the "real world". I tend to disagree with that way of teaching. Yes, the student must be "book smart", but more importantly to be financially successful, the student must be "money-smart". Educating kids about the importance of investing and how to handle this money once you make it, is lacking in our school system.

I believe that by teaching kids about investing at an early age, we will be teaching the kids to work smarter, not harder. By educating the kids on the ups and downs of the market, real estate transactions, mutual funds, bonds and many other investment vehicles, we will be teaching them something that they will know [and carry with them] for the rest of their life.

By also teaching these children about investing, we will also be teaching them that it is okay to make mistakes. Making mistakes and failing is the biggest lesson for any student or true investor. However, the school system looks at failure in a bad way. They expect the kids to be perfect and instill in these children a lifetime fear that if they do not do it perfectly every time, that it is not okay and they are failures, and this can lead to many problems. The school system should teach kids that failing is one of the biggest learning experiences a person can have, and that we learn greatly from our mistakes. This will allow children to feel okay about not having all of the answers or failing once in a while when they are adults in the real world, making real decisions.

I feel that investing and financial security should be one of the most emphasized subjects in high school. We should teach our children to work smarter, not harder. Let them feel okay about not having all the answers all the time. And most importantly, teach them something they can use in everyday life.

HIDDEN DIFFERENCES
HOW TO COMMUNICATE WITH GERMANS
(EXCERPT FROM AN ARTICLE)

This article came from <u>Stern</u> magazine (a German publication) regarding the differences between the two cultures. An understanding of the differences will aid in better communication. This article was written to help the business world understand each other better, but the basic tenets apply to anyone entering another's environment. The better armed we are, the better we can communicate. These are simply highlights from the article.

First, Americans are future-oriented. Partly this is due to our young age. Americans have not been around as long as the majority of the rest of the world. In Germany, they are past-oriented. They tend to want to start every conversation with some historical perspective. This leaves Americans cold because they simply want to get down to business.

> Americans are often accused of being superficial and lacking depth because they are impatient and have no time for historical perspective; they are interested only in the present. (Hall 20)

Also, Germans have some quiet time that is respected by everyone. In the afternoons, no one is allowed to run their lawn mowers or pound nails to disturb others. "There is no daily quiet time in America" (Hall 21).

In terms of time systems, there are monochromic and polyphonic time systems. These two systems are totally incompatible. Fortunately, Germans and Americans are part of the monochromic time systems, which means they can concentrate on only one thing at a time. When they are in a meeting, they are concentrated on the subject at hand and will ask to have no interruptions by means of calls or appointments. In a polyphonic time system, such as in the Latin American countries, all other things take precedence. Meetings and deadlines are often not adhered to and family and friends can happily sidetrack an important business meeting (Hall 22-23).

There is one myth that is inherent in America and that is that Americans feel they are a melting pot. In essence, we are. Immigrants make up this country and they hale from every conceivable part of the world. However, the chief founders of this country and the norm for all that is done here come from the Anglo Saxon lineage. Therefore, we tend to expect that others must acclimate to this predominantly Anglo-Saxon value system: one that values promptness and hard work. Now the face of America is changing and the values that have been expected for the last 200 years are being taken over by Latinos and others who come from a polyphonic time system and who value things quite opposite to the norms set up here. To succeed in America, immigrants are expected to adhere to these monochromic systems of interactions. If they do, they succeed at a much more remarkable rate. Will the Latino communities be able to stop this capitalistic march to the Anglo-Saxon tunes or will they, by sheer numbers, be able to turn the Anglo-Saxon tide to lighten up a bit? Could this be why the majority of Mexicans have failed to acclimate very well to this society, and are they waiting to overwhelm white America with their polyphonic ways?

However, we must return to the German culture, which, in many ways replicates our situation due to the vast numbers of immigrants in their own country. Germans are well known for promptness. They do not like you to be late to a meeting. They will immediately take it to mean that you are egocentric, rude, non-caring, or irresponsible. In a meeting, they approach the decisions more cautiously than Americans, and their planning is much lengthier, but once a decision is made, they stand behind it 100%. Yet in all their decision-making, they never forget the past. Their heritage, both the good and the bad, are carried with them like a badge of courage. This is tedious for Americans who believe the past is the past and that we just need to get on with it. Americans are always in a hurry to get things done. Let's not dwell on the past or recap last month's activities, let's just plan for the future (Hall 42-43).

Another major difference is the fact that Germans are far less mobile than Americans. They tend to stay in the same homes, often for generations, and in the same jobs. Whereas, Americans think nothing of moving to a new house every four or five years and just as frequently might look for another job. Also, Germans don't socialize as much with their neighbors or chat over the back hedges. They are more private and value their privacy more. They are also more distant in physical contact with each other. Americans tend to stand a lot closer when having a one-on-one conversation and Germans stand back more (Hall 44-47).

Americans tend to keep doors open, and Germans keep them closed. In a round robin discussion with a group of educators, they spoke about the bathroom door. When it is not in use, it is closed, and with Americans, it is left open. For Germans, "an open door seems sloppy and disorderly" (Hall 48).

Germans understand power and of all the five types of power: financial, entrepreneurial, political, managerial, and intellectual, they tend to value intellectual the most. They do not favor ostentatious displays of power, for position and success should be handled with grace and reserve (Hall 50-51).

As mentioned in other chapters, schools in Germany are compartmentalized and only academic subjects are taught. There are no clubs per se, and sports and other after school programs are pursued in the form of extracurricular activities (Hall 53). There are numerous extracurricular activities, done in the afternoons and weekends, such as pursuing theater, foreign languages, such as Spanish, Italian, Swedish, Dutch, or Russian. Student exchanges are very common with USA, France, Great Britain, Israel and since 1990, the Eastern Bloc countries, such as Czechoslavakia, Poland, Hungary, etc.

Germans tend to collect books for the sake of collecting, reading it later. Americans feel they need to read a book immediately. That is exactly why soft covered books sell more in the States and hard cover more in Germany. Germans have a need for a sense of permanence, due partly to their historic past. They see everything as having intrinsic value. That's why they have a reputation for high quality in their buildings, cars, furniture, and other possessions. They also do not believe in waste. They are appalled at the waste in America because they go to great lengths to recycle, and conserve heat and air and electricity. Never think of selling Germans shoddy goods. He will not tolerate it. This is exactly the reason why German cars are such high quality (Hall 54-56).

Germans are very conscious of good manners. "Educated, responsible people are expected to display good manners at all times" (Hall 57). This is why many Germans are uncomfortable with the casual way Americans have of referring to each other by first names when first being introduced. They have certain sayings at the table when eating and never forget anyone's birthday, which is often celebrated by bringing champagne and chocolates to work and splurging on a party for your co-workers. Their cordiality extends to references to family and friends, who send greetings and are reminders that others are mindful of thoughtfulness towards all acquaintances.

In general, Germans are better trained and better organized. A university degree means more than its equivalent in America because it entails much more time and effort (Hall 58). However, in this day and age, wealthy Germans are sending their children to private schools in America and onto American universities. They commonly send their children abroad to study, usually during the junior year, and then they may return there again for university.

Germans do not understand the way Americans compliment someone and then tell them what to improve upon. Germans are far more direct. "They rarely compliment someone on a job well done because they take it for granted that people will perform well . . . ." (Hall 60). This article was written in 1983, and since I was in Germany for the 1998-99 school year, I can see that some things that are in this report have changed somewhat. I think that Germans have adopted more American ways. This is something that many Germans often told me, with some sadness in the admittance. The baby boomer generation has changed the face of Germans and they look more and more like their American protégés. However, there are definite original German tendencies that linger.

Another important point in communicating with Germans is to give them more detailed background information than you are expected to give. Their language indicates this in a variety of ways. For example, in English we have one word for comfort, in the German language, they have eight, signifying a different type of comfort. Americans also like hype; and Germans avoid it. In a German meeting a soft-spoken person will hold the most power and one who makes a lot of noise will not be paid as much attention. In general, Americans tend to exaggerate things much more (Hall 61).

In regard to speaking their language, Germans really appreciate your attempts at speaking, and they're quite disturbed by your utter lack of interest in it (Hall 62). My experience has been that they find Americans extremely lazy and egocentric about learning others' languages. Since America is so large and English is the international language, many Americans do not see the necessity to learn a foreign language. Their arrogance extends to feeling that others should learn English and they have this expectation when traveling. As a consequence, the rest of the world does not disappoint Americans, as nearly everyone in Europe speaks English and most students have had at least six years of it in school.

Germans are extremely up front, serious about most things and often seem a bit aloof to Americans. They think that Americans are quite superficial and tend to remark on how our conversations tend to be rather full of fluff. They like to have philosophical conversations and enjoy having close friendships and bonds, but it just takes them longer to get to know you. They also "hate to make mistakes and become very upset when they do. They will not hesitate to tell you when you are out of line" (Hall 64-65). So, Americans have a tendency to be impatient about the getting-to-know-you process, and they jump to conclusions about the Germans' ability to be friendly. Essentially, "They don't show emotion but they feel it"(Hall 65). These traits are common for most Germans, although the face of youth will put yet another slant on the picture. With young kids both critical and admiring of the American scene, they will pick and choose what they like and end up with a uniquely German perspective, and that is how it should be.

HOMEROOM TEACHERS
THE TRUE LIFE PRESERVERS

The homeroom teacher has been together with the same class for 1-2 years and knows everything about each kid. When there is a personal problem with any one of them, the homeroom teacher is a good person with whom to touch base. She/he can clarify whatever the problem is and help the situation greatly.

The homeroom teacher meets with the same students regularly each week. They have a personal relationship with each one and good communication with the parents. They tutor, advise, conjole, and generally assist the student in every possible way. At grade conferences, this teacher represents each of his/her students and knows enough about each one so that background information can be provided, whenever needed. If another teacher is having trouble with the student or the student is not doing well in their class, the homeroom teacher can intercede. At any rate, the amount of time that each homeroom teacher spends with the same core group of kids is key to the success of this approach. There is less need of counselors or crisis intervention when a familiar adult is present in the child's life for a longer period of time.

Example: I had a twelfth grade kid who had missed 15 hours of class out of 45 due to a serious illness, but she never turned in any make-up work and when she came to ask me how she got her grade and I explained it to her, she was very unhappy. She then went to her homeroom teacher to complain and he saw me outside of class and asked for the details. After I told him the whole story, he understood and backed me up. This makes so much more sense. It also eliminates the need for a counselor.

IDEAL SCHOOL:
CALIFORNIA DREAMIN'

The all-important vital quotient in starting any new school is to have numbers that you can work with. I am a firm believer that it isn't the kids you have to work with as much as the size of the class. No, I take that back. There is one major factor in being able to be successful with kids. We must have some kind of screening process that involves not tests or intelligence factors or economic background, but <u>attitude</u>. If you have the right attitude in a child, you can accomplish absolutely anything. That child can be blind, deaf, black, white, or purple and you will have success. So, combine these two factors and voila! You have a successful school.

The concentration in the regular high school should be <u>all</u> college bound students in intensive courses like we now have, except the recipients will be students who are comfortable being there, and have a positive attitude.

The rest of the students, who are not comfortable with the college bound curriculum, can be linked up with the junior college as early as freshman year. If we follow the general idea of the German system, we could have the freshmen try out 2-3 weeks of some kind of training they could get in a class at the junior college. When coordinating it with the college, these classes could be in the morning so kids could go directly there from home and be bussed back to class for the afternoon or arrange for them to stay the day and explore more than one subject area. This would be repeated at the end of the year, as well.

By sophomore year, they could decide what they like best in the vocations, and take one class there. By junior year, they could be doing morning or afternoon classes, and senior year, whatever fits their schedule, so that they could then complete only a semester or one year at college to be certified after graduation.

The most ideal would be to build a vocational school instead of another high school. I know the cost would be far more than a conventional school but it could serve a number of communities. This is exactly what is being done in New Hampshire, where their tech school is utilized by several high schools in the area.

However, since the cost is a factor, why not use our local junior college, which already has programs in place?

Partnerships

A Regatta Race

In order for the school system to prosper, we must have partnerships between every aspect of the community, administrators, teachers, parents, students, and at every level of learning. That means it must start at the kindergarten level and be consistently adhered to throughout a child's primary, middle, and high school years. Feedback on a regular basis will be what we use to constantly improve the system. The component parts are: parents, students, primary schools, middle schools, high school teachers, community college, special programs, government programs, administration, business, community and aides.

To start with, I would like to see two kinds of parent groups. Like one on parenting, where we offer on-going weekly parenting classes that inform parents as to what they can do to help their son or daughter. Things that should be covered are: time management skills, designated time and place to work each night, organizational skills that include keeping a date book and a binder. This meeting could also cover scholarship availability and the need for long-term planning for their child in regard to what classes to take and what extracurricular activities to be involved in. Here we could reinforce the need for consistent discipline in doing their homework and having it checked by them on a regular on-going basis. There should be translators there for Spanish, Mien, Hmong, and whatever other languages are needed.

Last year, I conducted just such meetings over a three-week period. They were hour-long sessions in which I covered exactly how the class was set up and what they could do at home to help me. I was able to reach 50 parents. These were the parents whose kids were getting either a D or F. It helped for a while and made me feel like I had done my part in trying to enlist their help and have them feel included. Then we need feedback to know what else we need to do in the future. I had contracts signed by parents and students to make sure all parties understood what was expected.

The second part of the parent quotient is to have them included in all general meetings, including the faculty meeting. A parent representative from each of the different language groups could be there and then they could pass on this information to designated smaller groups of teachers that meet continuously all year. We need a leader for the Asian and Spanish communities that could help to organize that.

Next, students need to feel more included by being part of these same meetings. They would attend faculty meetings, help with the disciplining of students, and be on a committee to represent homerooms. These homerooms would be established in the freshmen year with the same homeroom teacher staying with them all four years. We already have student council meetings where reps are involved, but we need to establish more concrete, close-knit groups. Young people need to feel committed to their school and if they don't have a say, they will not care. There needs to be more peer evaluations allowed where peers can get feedback from peers. A peer-tutoring program should also be set up. Feedback should be elicited from the kids on a regular basis. Once a week meetings should be held. Students can help with program development. They have creative and innovative ideas and know what they want to learn. Let them also have the reins.

At the primary level, homeroom situations can be set up then. If they have the same teacher for the first few minutes of the day for all seven years, there will be some proper bonding with an influential adult. At middle school, it continues for two more years, and then the last four with another set of teachers. The Germans employ this method and it works really well. What is of utmost importance is coordination between primary and middle and middle and high school so the transition will be smoother. That will entail appointing liaisons that will work with the previous school to assure a smooth transition. However, it must be ongoing with monthly collaboration or it will not work.

Between high school and junior college, so much more can be done. Upper level kids are already taking college classes to enhance their GPA in the academic areas. Why not let us develop a vocational component, where hands-on kids can take vocational classes and coordinate it with their high school requirements so they can be certified in a field of their interest and employable by the end of their high school years. It could operate the same as with the AP kids, giving everyone more options. There are so many rich programs already existing at the college that have certification programs. Why aren't we telling kids about them and managing a way for them to be involved before they get totally turned off by the tenth or eleventh grade. Kids only hear about college and for those kids who don't particularly like the idea of college because they want to learn a trade, it is a big turn-off. In other words, we need to provide more options for kids and let them know there are other ways to approach their education.

The government, as I mentioned before, tend to throw out new ideas, but they are so numerous in number and so diverse in ideology, that it becomes one giant jigsaw puzzle, as one journalist put it. (See Jigsaw Puzzle chapter.) School to Work Opportunities Act was one idea; then School to Career (basically the same but renamed); even apprenticeships have been bandied about. Almost anyone with good writing skills can apply for a grant to support any project that the government deems worthy in a desperate attempt to improve the system. However, there are too many disjointed parts to this educational puzzle, that experts are needed just to keep abreast of the latest magic pill. We need someone to sort through programs and stick with the same approach long enough to acclimate teachers and students and then allow it to work. Government, however, cannot make up its mind. I strongly advocate that government funding goes to the local businesses to encourage them to support the school systems.

Administration, at present, is walking a tightrope between keeping abreast of the myriad changes in policy and funding, while having their jobs threatened if they can't produce passing scores for their kids. Guidance counselors are so overloaded, they can't be truly effective in giving advice or scheduling classes. Everyone is so stressed out that no one can do an effective job. Don't you think kids pick up on that? Their frustrations stem from our frustrations. Yet, they have no place to vent it because they have no say in what happens to them.

Next, businesses in any community are key to the success of kids. If the government spends half of its education money in support of programs to encourage business people to start apprenticeship programs, we would be headed in a positive direction. Right now, we have a tiny portion of the school population involved with shadowing and mentoring programs, and our own Regional Occupational Program and Work Experience Program do an excellent job of supporting kids in a practical way. However, there are far too many kids unaware of these programs or not encouraged to utilize them. If we had more kids in it, we wouldn't have the teachers to cover it or the funds to support more classes like it. It is designed for a finite number of kids. We are grossly underrepresented with this program. We could also enlist the support of major corporations such as IBM, Mackintosh, and Hewlett Packard to support us in a variety of ways. Since technology is developing at the pace it is, computers become obsolete before you can say Jack Robinson. Those computers can be passed on to schools that aren't as up-to-date.

In addition to businesses, the general public can be called on to speak. Many volunteers have already given their time and many are willing to do more. Organizations like Rotary, the Chamber of Commerce, Toastmasters, Lions, Kiwanis, AAUW (Association of University Women) and many more, offer opportunities for young people in all aspects of leadership roles. They are happy to be involved. Furthermore, there are parents and retired people willing to come into class and spend time with kids and help teachers. Kids need to be exposed to all aspects of society, not isolate themselves and be beholden to just teachers. Education is not just four walls of the classroom; we need to bring the world in.

Our schools do have some wonderful programs and some phenomenal teachers. Some of these have already been mentioned. Some of them should be cloned, such as the agriculture program, AVID, a program designed to promote college for out-of-mainstream-kids, ROP, Work Experience, CAD Training, Career Center, Computer Technology and numerous others. The problem is we need to make these programs more accessible to kids.

To further these partnerships, we have to have a full time faculty member or other qualified personnel to coordinate these programs. It is not enough to have someone at the district office, there needs to be a liaison in each school, talking with the public, coordinating speaking engagements, scheduling meetings, providing feedback, and giving speeches to local businesses and organizations.

"IN GOOD COMPANY"

They sit there
The subjects of my dreams
Cursing
Muttering
And loathsome
Of me.

I mean no more to them
Than a roll of toilet paper entangling the chair leg
Or a tack on a chair
Or a hostile stare.
They use me
Abuse me
And accuse me of educating them

"Why is this wrong?!" they scream.
"This assignment wasn't late!" they entreat.
"You lost my paper!" they accuse.

Day by day
Piece by piece
They take a little bit of me
They chew it up

And spit it out!

But it's my choice to teach
And instead of a congregation
I have an amalgamation of fools . . . I'm in good company!

FROM JIGSAW PUZZLE TO MERRY-GO-ROUND

(EXCERPT FROM AN ARTICLE)

"The state's elaborate system of public school standards, tests and other reforms resembles "pieces of a jigsaw puzzle just dumped from the box," says a new study" ("Study" A4)

This statement perfectly depicts what I have been up against as a teacher for years. The government never gives us a chance to see if one idea, strategy, ideology, concept, philosophy, belief, or principle will actually work. They simply throw big money at us until the money runs out and we have to run with the bucks until the idea fades due to lack of funds. We tend to go in two to three year spurts before money dries up and new ideas flourish. In any new business, it takes three to five years to make a go of it. You cannot expect instant returns with so little time commitment in any endeavor you pursue. The article goes on to say, according to University of California, Berkeley, and Stanford University, that the number of reforms being handed down sends mixed signals to teachers. Elizabeth Burr, co-author of the report by Policy Analysis for California Education urges leaders in Sacramento to alter the pace and work more slowly at improving the schools day by day. Some of the many new reforms proposed in the last couple of years by two California governors are:

1) Income tax exemptions for teachers;
2) Internet classroom connections;
3) A variety of incentive "carrots" for low-performing schools;
4) A high school graduation test;
5) Ranking all schools according to test scores;
6) Putting 430 schools through a three year improvement program;
7) Counseling and reviewing colleagues' performance;
8) Class size reduction in primary grades;
9) Tough standards outlining what kids should learn; and
10) A standardized statewide test. ("Study" A4)

I have to add to this what has recently transpired in the Bay Area. There the starting salaries went up by $10,000 and no-interest loans are being offered to certain district teachers to purchase a home. In our own district, the 99-2000 salaries went up by 11.3%. So, there is a desperate need to find a way to improve the system. They have also discussed the possibility of merit pay, but the teachers' association is dead-set against it because the system can be so easily abused. Also, school vouchers went on the ballots in 2000, but were defeated. This is government's attempt to subsidize parents in educating their kids at private schools that are run by non-credentialed staff with a select entry policy that excludes all but the narrow type of kid wanted in a school of dubious curriculum and background. It is like government is thrashing around in the dark searching for solutions, but the mental groping is doing nothing to better the conditions of kids in public high schools. Stop the merry-go-round, I want off!

JUST ANOTHER PERSPECTIVE
STUDENT ESSAY: BY MAI VANG
CLASS OF 2003

This is an example of the types of student writing I deal with everyday. This is part of their heritage and the concerns they carry with them into the classroom.

Vietnam War

One day I was bored and my dad told my whole family to come and he would tell us a story about the Vietnam War. The story was so scary and creepy. The story lasted three hours.

It all started at the farm where they worked. Okay, I will recall everything they did. Well, my mom went first and my dad came last. My mom left before my dad. It took 45 minutes to get to the farm. When she got there, she started to work. Then about one and a half hours later, my dad came and helped my mom. They were working for a long time until this one man from the village came and told them that there were some weird looking people coming to our village and taking all the men.

When my mom and dad heard about it, they left everything at the farm. They took off and ran to their home and told everybody that there were Vietnamese people coming to our village and they were trying to take all the men. My mom and everybody at the village started to pack everything, and they took off running to the forest. The entire family was scared to death. Most of the babies were crying so hard that some of the people were going to kill their own child. Then they found a place to build some banana leaf homes. All the Hmong people were so hungry.

They spent the night in the forest. They were so hungry, that they starved to death. They had nothing to eat. The only thing they had was banana roots and bananas. All the babies could not stop crying; they cried all night long. Some people did not get to sleep because they were scared and they didn't want to die. When they were sleeping, they heard a noise out in the forest. Then everybody started to cry and run. They ran as fast as they could, but some people were left behind. So, some people were being killed and some were not. They ran until they got to a quiet place. But the only thing in the way was the children and the babies. The babies were crying so much that one of my dad's friends had to kill their own child. This was the only way to keep them safe. Some people were safe and some were not because they got lost in the forest. My dad told me that he was lucky because he and my mom did not get killed. This Vietnam War was the worst thing that ever happened to the Hmong people.

I'm so happy that we are in the U.S. and not in Laos again. I'm glad that my mom and dad are living with us today and forever. They mean everything to me. I'm so sorry for the other people that were there in the Vietnam War. The only one I want to thank is God. He saved my parents, brothers, and me. He was the one who took care of us and took us to the U.S. He will always be in my family and within me. Thank you, God, for being there and helping my family. You mean so much to us.

KINDS OF KIDS
FROM SURFERS TO SEASONED SAILORS

What kind of kids are we dealing with on a regular basis? There are several categories that they come in. Nerds, Jocks, Stoners, Ravers, Gang Wannabees (GW's), Gang Bangers (GB's), Punks, I-Don't-Givashitters (IDG's), Preppies, Over-Achievers, Fall-Thru-the-Crackers (FTTC's), Clowns, Gothics, and Blades, just to name a few.

Let's start with Nerds. Nerds have been around for centuries. Stereotypically, a nerd wears horn-rimmed glasses and is preoccupied with mechanical devices. Of course, in this day and age of computers, the Computer Nerd is to be found almost everywhere. In fact, it is almost a fashion statement to be called a computer nerd. They are in the greatest demand. Every classroom teacher would give their right arm to have a true Computer Nerd in their classroom. He is the one who can answer all those tricky questions regarding the how and why of computer operation at the flick of a switch or a dot com command. Kids tend to vie for this position and it ends up going to the kid that ultimately has the most and latest knowledge. Every year, teachers get on their knees and pray for such a kid.

Jocks are the next on the list and they have also been around as long as schools have existed. The quintessential jock has at least three distinct sports that he is interested in, so he can play fall, winter, and spring. So, he starts with football in the fall, after heavy-duty workouts and practices in the summer months. That means they start the school year in full swing to begin the serious climb to state finals by the end of the season. Every jock's dream is to be on that winning team and to work up to varsity star linebacker by their senior year, which may guarantee a four-year scholarship to a university of their choice. A super jock continues the year in wrestling for the winter sport, and ends it with baseball for the spring. Nowadays, if a super jock is also academically strong, he is practically guaranteed a full scholarship. How do others view these jocks? Needless to say, the girls are wild about those rippling muscles and firm biceps and never fail to salivate for an invitation to any one of the yearly school dances. Teachers often find jocks a bit deficient in some academic areas, but their charming self-confidence makes up for the loss, unless their ego is just too enormous to make him palatable to anyone. That seldom happens because teenagers let each other know, right quick, just what a jerk everyone thinks someone else is.

The problem is usually not with jocks, but their coaches. Imagine having a star player on your team. He is someone who is an invincible super player who consistently scores way above the norm nearly every game. He is a player who generates a glorious hope to score on top in the state finals, who makes the heart of the coach beat extra fast each time he sees him make that play. Grades come out and the jock is failing one too many classes. What is there to do? Well, the great debate is whether the coach can remain still and let things be, or if he has to manifest some change by virtue of 1) changing a grade himself clandestinely; or 2) pressuring a teacher to change a grade. It's a huge moral dilemma for everyone involved. Of course, if it's an English teacher, with no interest in anything outside of Shakespeare and Chaucer, the morality issue is an out-and-out perversion of principles. If the academic teacher is a coach himself/herself or takes a big interest in that particular sport, you may have a good team of players in this game of subterfuge. This moral chess game takes place year after year, time after time, as the age-old saga of jock versus academics continue to battle against the state champion odds. Only you can be the judge as to whether the moral war is ever won.

Next, come the Stoners, and since drugs have been around since the sixties, at least in the form of marijuana, it is somewhat of an old hat thing. However, since the sixties, the drug of choice has changed. Now, the millennium Stoners prefer designer drugs, often named after famous people, like Calvin Klein. These are drugs that are often found at raves, (Ravers will be discussed later). Stoners generally come in a couple of different forms. Those kids who just do marijuana, and those who go in for the more hard core crack cocaine versions. The typical Stoner may be a kid who is much more mature than others and sets himself apart through drugs. He is literally escaping, like the good ole days when that was the only way you could "groove". Other kids may not be as recognizable and may be getting it from their addicted parents or an older sibling. Nonetheless, when we talk about it in class, kids tell me it is everywhere and easy to procure. We still have our undercover narcs, who are grown-up cops posing as a kid. They enroll in school and just blend in with the others to uncover drug rings in the school. That will often put a temporary halt to some of the drug shenanigans.

However, a temporary halt is all we can hope for, so we, as teachers, are warned to be aware of the telltale signs of drug use. A slip in grades, mood swings, frequent absences, lack of homework or a sudden change in doing their work is certainly an indication of something unusual going on. However, many kids display those very traits on a daily basis and it can be chalked up to indifference and/or laziness. Then again, occasionally, we identify serious problems. This year, on the first day of school, one of my students just vomited in class. Come to find out she had gotten drunk before school even started and then got sick when she got to school. She was so distraught she begged me not to tell anyone. By the time I did report it, she was off campus and I was reprimanded for not letting the vice-principal know about it soon enough. Another student had such dramatic mood swings and inconsistent attendance and performance that when we had a meeting with all his teachers and his parents, we found out that he <u>was</u> on drugs.

In the same realm as the Stoners, we see Ravers who spend their weekends at raves. This is a dance place from hell, where girls get slipped drugs in their drinks and end up being raped before the night is over. Where the latest in drugs are offered the minute you walk into the room, where the lights are strobes and the bodies are gyrating to a drugged out beat, and where total decadence and brain decay lay waste to our youth. "A June 18, [2000] rave dubbed "Metropolis" held at the Santa Clara County Fairgrounds resulted in two stabbings, eight arrests and at least 12 people treated for drug-related problems (Monterey County Herald 7/9/2000 B5). These kids often look like any others, but their grades are sometimes among the lowest. They live for the weekend and that psychedelic high, and eventually their behaviors take a cumulative toll on their lives.

Another rather small but unique group of kids is the Punks or Punk Rockers. Mohawks, piercings, tattoos, tattered clothes and colored hair, styled in a mad array of wildness, characterize them. It might be half shaved, sticking straight up and out or completely bald. I once had a preppie type student go Mohawk. He considered himself an undercover Punk, just to get people's reactions. Skinheads, who tried to recruit him at parties, often approached him. He was very pleased to tell the Skinheads exactly what he thought of them, in his quiet, pleasing voice that probably left them stone faced as he walked away. Looks are deceiving and a lot of youth try on images for a while just to get our reactions. Punks are relatively benign and stick to their own. Many were intellectually in the class with Gothics, who felt they were trying to make the same kind of statement in their quiet, introspective way. In a TV report in July 2000, a Jock was tried in the death of a Punk when they ended up in an altercation. Here we have two distinctly different teenagers, who might as well live on different planets when it comes to social interactions.

Sometimes, so-called Stoners may turn to gang banging or just fall into the more benign category of Gang Wannabees. Sometimes gangbanging turns into a convenient, fast moneymaking scheme to subsidize their cohorts in drugs. In our little town of 60,000, there are at least forty identified gangs of all colors and signs. The clothes they wear characterize them, but now that has become a fashion statement too. The loose baggy pants with roomy elongated pockets were convenient for storing weapons. The long over-sized shirts helped to hide any further bulk. However, the Bladers took over their countenance because it was easier to skate in loose clothes. Of course, the Gang Wannabees took on the clothes code so they could look the part. Both the actual Gang Bangers and the Wannabees take on gestures and language much like their rap song heroes and the violent lyrics of those songs pump up and support their sense of the uselessness of mankind. Their attitudes are reflected in their behavior at school, which is a vehement dislike for anything useful in life. They are the biggest class disrupters on a daily basis because they hold nothing to be sacred outside the codes of their gang members' torrid existences.

In the same category as the GW's and GB's, are the I-Don't-Giveashitters. Only these kids take pride in non-associations. They are in a class by themselves because of their total indifference. They think nothing of telling you to go straight to hell or openly calling you a few more choice names in front of the class. You can throw them out and they strut out proudly, usually announcing their tremendous pleasure in doing so. They are also disdainful of all others except their prototypes. They pride themselves in being able to elicit racial slurs at the slightest provocation. They love to use their race as an excuse for being treated unfairly, at least in terms of punishment for their anti-social behavior. Otherwise, they are quick to remind everyone around them that they are superior and they better not find anyone "dissing" them.

On the opposite scale, there are Preppies and Over-Achievers, who are somewhat similar, sometimes even synonymous. Over-achievers can come in all shapes and sizes. They are the ones that have over a 100% average and will squabble over 2 points taken away on a homework assignment worth 100 points, when their overall grade encompasses 7000 points for the semester. They assiduously check every detail of the assignment you give back to see if you made a mistake. They do exactly what you tell them all to do, but because there are so few kids who do it, you find their nit picking annoying. In retrospect, I am glad they care that much because they represent less than 4 % of our total student population.

While Over-Achievers can be any kind of kid regardless of race or economic background, Preppies are generally all white, upper middle class kids. They are the ones who run for offices in the student council, they are taking early morning studies either to get ahead on credits or in an accelerated program of studies or as part of the music program. We have pockets of kids who even attend bible studies at 6 am each morning before they come to school. (I personally find this training admirable.) They are also often involved in a chosen sport and in numerous club activities. This well-rounded student is the classic example of careful planning by the parents. These parents are also well educated and intend to utilize all the advantages of the system and let their son or daughter's resume speak for itself when scholarship time comes around. They often dress in designer polo shirts and tailored shorts. They are clean cut and neat in appearance, and often what lurks behind that façade is an anxious teenager with a lot on his/her plate, under a lot of pressure to turn out a 4.4 grade point average. Those kids represent 2-4% of the entire student body in our school and they <u>do</u> go off to university directly after high school. Some may even have completed the first year of college before they graduate from high school, due to their rigorous schedules, which often includes taking junior college courses during their junior/senior years.

The question is, what price do the parents pay for over-scheduled, regimented, stressed out kids before they even move on to university? That may be the reason why some get involved with alcohol and drugs and burn out the first year of college. Be that as it may, these parents are a force to reckon with if your curriculum of study is not what they expect it to be. Or if the teacher gives a grade lower than a B, those parents will come storming into the school and demand to know why. One of our teachers was caught in this dilemma when she accused an AP (advanced placement) student of plagiarism. It often ends up in a witch-hunt against the teacher, with support from other AP parents, who always associate with each other, especially over common school issues. I was victimized by a number of these types of students when teaching a course. When one or more of these students do not like you for whatever reason, that disregard gets passed from one family to another. Soon, the collaboration between parents end up in phone calls where the principal is called and that is the end of your career in that field. I was reassigned due to the lack of support from this dominant social group. So, dealing with the Preppies is a mixed bag. On one hand, there is an enormous pleasure in dealing with sophisticated students who care deeply about their studies and will do more than assigned. However, the down side is the relentless pressure you feel from the parents if you do anything short of pleasing them or pleasing their offspring should these kids consider you less than worthy or just don't like your style of teaching.

Another type of student that I strive to assist all during the year, are the Fall-Thru-the-Crackers. These kids are often mediocre to bad students, (for any number of reasons) and sit at their desk, quietly failing. You make phone calls home, have parent conferences, console, coerce and otherwise try every trick in the book to get a response from them. After a certain period of time, (I usually give up after the first four months), they simply slide very quietly between the cracks and die a slow academic death that ends up in summer school, where they have succeeded in working the system again. I mean, think about it. Who wouldn't want to spend 20 hours a week for six weeks, working on an academic class that can be completed before you can say Jack Robinson. It is just a long drawn-out painful experience for parents and teachers to try to keep them on task when they have already opted for summer school (in their mind) after the first quarter. Summer school is used for two types of students: the Preppies and Over-Achievers to stay ahead of the game, and the FTTC's, who know that they can be lazy and irresponsible and laid back during the school year because summer school looms ahead. Their attitude is . . . "as long as I pass, I am happy". Unfortunately, many students fall into this category during the year, and are jubilant to know they did not fail, which is usually by a percent of a percentage point.

On the lighter side, Clowns have been around for centuries. In fact, after they get a clue about your boundaries, they are rather nice to have around. Nearly every class has one and they are notorious for major disruptions the first few weeks of class. They are born stand-up comedians, and always volunteer to be up front in charge of something. They often appear to be ADD kids; they can't stay in their seats, and make theatrics out of even the simplest thing. Every paper to be thrown away is a basket to make, wadded up nicely, with the arm pulled back tight and then Swoosh! It lands in or at the side of the trashcan. It is always accompanied by a wallop! Or yeow! In the middle of an explanation of some important point. Of course, all students begin guffawing and snorting laughter, while I vacillate between ushering him out the door (because it is the fifth time that period that he has disrupted my class) or I could simply ignore him again. He doesn't walk back to his seat, he slides or moonwalks or hip hops back with a foolish grin on his face. Always wishing to be the center of attention, he makes it impossible to teach, until, of course, he is sent to the office one time too many. Or after several phone calls home, with continuous lamentations by the parents, who know their child well, and can often chronicle the course of his antics dating back to Kindergarten. After the Clowns mellow out, they can actually be fun to have in the room, but Clowns need to be tamed.

Another rather benign group are the Bladers. They live to roller blade or skateboard. They are really rather a devoted, talented group, focused on what has become a competitive sport. They sometimes bring their boards or blades to school and practice at lunch or arrive and depart on their mobile units. They are pretty wholesome kids and seldom cause problems.

Last, there are the Gothics. Now, on the level of medieval studies, they are the most interesting kids. I have often admired them on the basis of bringing back to life an ancient culture. Although "gothic" has a pretty ominous meaning in today's context of words. It is described as wild, uncivilized, uncivil, savage, rude, barbarous, barbaric, and barbarian. Perhaps that is the reason they wear all black. The girls sometimes wear long vampire-like capes and their lipstick and other make-up is black. They are often extremely bright and mature beyond their years. They often write poetry and are contemplative and introspective and quiet. They make a statement with their clothes, but they do not make trouble.

Yet, teaching all these kinds of kids helps to open up new worlds to me. I appreciate them and find them endlessly fascinating. So, when you think of educating young people, you are looking at a microcosm of the world, not a stamped-out prototype that responds to the same set of SAT tests and ACT exams. Each comes from a different perspective, with different expectations from the parents and different values at home, and different feelings and urges. All these aspects must be appreciated to develop the whole child. No one set of criteria for judging both teachers and student performance can truly identify what the problem is. We need to examine a variety of so-called "norms" to get this country re-educated. Norms that pertain to race, color, creed, economic background, region of the country, local and state mandates, and level of intelligence in education.

LIFE'S GATEWAY

As you travel through life's way
It won't be hard to forget what I say

Like, "Quiet! Order! Don't talk back!"
And, "It's only adverbs that you lack!"

But also, try to see the light
A never-ending pure delight

Of fancy dances
Sporty cars

And wondering if you will ever get far.

Of all the good things
Bright & new

That keep on always happening to you.

For never will you pause again
At life's gateway to woman and man!

So, try to remember along the way
I may be awful on certain days

But in my heart, I love you true
And only want what's best for you!

MAINE SCHOOL: A MODEL

(EXCERPT FROM ARTICLE)

Inspired by educators, parents, and students, a new school was developed in Kennebunkport, Maine. It opened in September 2000. These were the tenets they set up to be fulfilled:

1) To take an active role in the community and school
2) Learn to govern themselves
3) Determine school policies
4) Work collaboratively with administrators, teachers, and community
5) Create a unique, multi-disciplinary learning environment. (Brockway)

As of February 2001, there were only 15 students, but they wish to enlarge their school by 150. Students come from diverse economic and philosophical backgrounds. These are the types of students that we see everyday in public schools. Kids who are bright but bored, kids with disabilities, and kids who were tired of being lost in the shuffle. However, all students were willing to work hard, take a chance on something new, and celebrate their differences (Brockway).

The courses are Maine-certified and accredited class work. Their elective classes are selected independently and involve the community:

They study astronomy at night under the stars of West Kennebunk. They study river ecology, along the banks of the Kennebunk River. They study German by immersing themselves in a German high school for three weeks overseas. Physical fitness includes yoga, spinning and health club workouts with area businesses. (Brockway)

They display their work at an open house, where they discuss, at length, their myriad projects with the sophistication of a college grad. They also help to maintain the school by working on the maintenance, running fundraisers, and helping with the selection of courses, faculty reviews, and all other aspects of running an institute of learning.

At planning meetings, all voices are heard and all people are respected equally. These students have absolute control over what they learn (Brockway). Could we learn something from them? Think about it.

MIRRORS OF OUR LIFE

A street light
Soaks
The golden tree.
Dark silhouettes
Reach to the sky
Deep puddles of delight
Sparkle, glitter
Soaking up the soft moonlight.
The surface mirror
Exchanging
Thoughts,
The warmth undulates,
The sweaty bodies
Reaching out
Grasping, grabbing
Skimming the surface
Moving, pulsating
Intruding on my silence.
Puddle-collecting
Around the surface
Of my mind.
Playing tunes as voices lift
To the jesters of the sky.

Chaperoning a school dance . . .
A crowded room for contemplation

MULTIPLE INTELLIGENCES
FROM BEACHCOMBERS
TO CRUISE SHIP CAPTAINS

I mentioned in a previous chapter that my kids are all gifted in a major way. Just because they do not excel in English doesn't mean they are not gifted. Each child has a gift from God and I feel it is my job to help identify it and strengthen and encourage it. That is why when Howard Gardner's book, <u>Frames of Mind: The Theory of Multiple Intelligences</u>, came out in 1983, it definitely answered a lot of questions for me about why my kids did or did not do much work for me in English. You see I believe that if we offered courses in English, focused on a particular theme/study, there would be much bigger buy-in on the part of the kids. For example, we have an incredibly strong agricultural program (talked about in a previous chapter), which is taught on another campus where I taught English for three years. I mentioned teaching this class as an Ag English class, focused on ag subjects for the writing and reading. All other English classes could also be set up that way: scientific English, business English, math English,

Historic English, aligned with the history curriculum, etc. As long as kids are reading and writing, why is it necessary to study Shakespeare and Chaucer? You can teach them critical thinking skills much more easily when they have it aligned with their curricular choices.

Let's take a look at the multiple intelligences. A **linguistic** child is very verbal, loves to talk in front of groups, will likely be in drama and public speaking classes. They are verbose by

98

nature. They are also the more aggressive ones who are not afraid to speak up to the teacher. They are so articulate that you often feel you are taking a back seat to their abilities. They are the ones who will head up the group work.

Next, you have the **logical-mathematical**. These tend to be the boys more than the girls. They have a more logical approach to the way they learn. That's why poetry seems so superfluous to them. You don't see any real order in it. At least not free verse. Some of my mathematical geniuses could identify with a sonnet that had more specific structure or Haikus that followed a distinct pattern. However, most discussions of literature were just a bit much for their liking.

Next, is **musical**. This is the student who always has a tune in his head, who bee bops when he walks in the room. He loves to bring you music to play and swears it is the greatest song ever. He can lip sync like a pro, may play an instrument or sing, and often gets really turned on when doing poetry, especially when the unit is introduced with the use of contemporary songs. They are easily inspired to write their own lyrics. It often helps if they have just had a personal heartbreak.

Next, there is **spatial intelligence**, which is the ability to see in pictures. These kids often graffiti up their notebooks, love to write on the board, can be an excellent artist already, and when given the slightest encouragement, can produce any kind of a project with panache. Their cover page on the poetry project is a masterpiece of color and style, which is often carried throughout the whole project.

Next, **bodily kinesthetic**, this person cannot sit still. They are often good athletes, actors, and dancers. They come to class with a bounce in their step; some cannot stay in their seat very long. When asked to participate in front of the class, they are the first to volunteer. They like to goof off, tell jokes, get a laugh, run the class, and try to tell me what to do!

Next, there is **interpersonal**. This loquacious person not only likes others and seems to have a lot of friends, they also have a sixth sense about people. This kind of kid will walk in; take a look at me and can read my mood like a book. The first words out of his/her mouth is whether I am having a good day or not, and if not, they want to know everything about it. He/she is the kid who gives you compliments and hugs you for no reason at all. The kid who writes you a note or tells you about their latest adventure when they think you have time to listen because they can also sense when you are too busy or stressed out.

Next, appears **intrapersonal**. These students have the same perceptions and feelings as the interpersonal kid, but they don't yet know how to utilize it. They are the kids who never say a word all year and then write an essay with the depth of an experienced wise old man or woman. They may whisper with their friends in class, but never trust themselves to speak out in class or come in front to give a talk. Yet, they are deeply sensitive to others. They simply observe and digest quietly.

Last, there is a new category, the **naturalist**, who can categorize, memorize, and understand complex structures. This person can rattle off the tenets of fascism, recall all the prepositions in the correct alphabetical order, and knows every planet in the universe and how many moons it has, can tell you historical data dating back to the Anglo-Saxon Period, and will gladly memorize a poem or short story that is assigned.

So, how do we meet the needs of all these different intelligence levels? We have to vary the curriculum and our approach to it. We have to reach beyond the comfort area of our own strengths and venture into some of their strengths. There are times when I am reminded of how little I know in comparison to some of my students. So, I try to remind them of how good they are at other subjects, if they don't feel successful in English.

NEVER NEVER LAND OF EDUCATION
A FEW DAYS IN AUGUST & SEPTEMBER 2000

This chapter chronicles the daily or weekly issues in Golden Valley High School located in Merced, California. The demographics are about 60% Hispanic, 25% Asian, 10% White, 5% Black/Other. We live in a poor economic region in valley farmland in a community of about 60,000. There are (as of August 2000) 51 identified gangs in Merced County, of which 1,024 young people are members. We also have a rather large Mormon community and a good portion of the 10% Whites are in this group in school. They are the Advance Placement kids. So, we have the two extremes and every conceivable mix in between those two enclaves. My attempt is to provide the daily activities in the school from as many perspectives as possible. I wish to include my thoughts, feelings, frustrations, and the way my students feel about it, as well. There needs to be a change in American education and perhaps we can start here.

August 21, 2000

Before school ever started, I was given a rough estimate of 183 students to start. We received a raise this year of 11.3% and (apparently) had a choice to reduce the numbers in class or get the raise. Since so many of my colleagues are close to retirement, they chose to take the raise. Consequently, our student numbers are all high. It is ironic that we greedily take the salary so we can retire with more money, and we may never retire at all due to the stress of our workload. We lost two teachers last year from strokes. One healthy 60 year old low key person collapsed in class and died a day or two later. Another was a 51-year-old male who died suddenly while shooting the breeze with his cronies. He had a particularly bad year where he was accused of something that ruined his previously good reputation. Many people feel he ultimately died from the stress of that ordeal.

This year's workload was double what I had last year. I was on a smaller campus, and I started out with 125 students, which later dropped to 96. That is a reasonable load. Even with that lighter load, I had a disproportionate number of "F's". How was I going to fare this year with twice the load?

The first day was hectic, as always. There is so much to get ready ahead of time, and it seems you always leave things out. Spread out all the handouts on the counter and have the kids collect them as they come in. Explain the course and expectations. My concentration the first day was to make sure all the parents knew that I was having a meeting the first two weeks of school. Back to School Night in September always has such an abysmal turn-out that I thought meetings held right after the start of school would work out better.

August 22

Second day of class. On this day, you begin to see the kids coming out of their quiet mode. The loud mouths cannot be quiet more than one day. I gave more explanations of what to do on their assignments. Many seniors brought in their meeting notices. I was to meet with parents that night. By the end of the last period I had a huge load of work to correct and sat there until 6:30 that night to finish it. I had a meeting with senior parents from 7-8:30 that was a big success. There were 15 parents there and a few of my students, as well. I will insert the agenda here to show you what I covered. I felt that rapport was established and we all left on a positive note.

August 23

Third day of class. Still collecting notices for the meeting tonight. In one of my sophomore classes, we discussed the lyrics of a popular song by TLC, called "No Scrubs". It was a very interesting discussion because it was on the level of the kids' interest. The word, "ghetto" came up and we started to discuss the gang situation in Merced. I shared the statistics with them and made a few funny/sarcastic remarks about gang members. There were several Asian boys in that class and I thought to myself that I was probably setting myself up for trouble by heavy-handing the kids too much. I jokingly talked about not taking a contract out on me. "Raise your hands now and say, 'I will not take out a contract on Mrs. Strauss!'"

After class, I ran into our campus police officer who had given me those statistics, and he said that I do have to tread lightly with that subject. That is what we are up against in schools today. There is the ever-present threat of danger. My students have even started writing about that and how they do not feel safe here. That night I had 19 more senior parents at the meeting and it went really well. That day I actually had time to have dinner before the meeting.

Reflections: What if we were offered $1000.00 to the teacher who gets the most parents to meet with them in the first four weeks of school, which would include Back to School Night. I firmly agree that getting to know the parents and forming what I call an alliance with each other helps to get these kids through the year. Also, psychologically, kids who know that you are meeting with their parents seem to take their studies a bit more seriously. Of course, there are still 71 kids who did not return the notice to be signed. Those will be the kids who don't do well in school and don't want to let their parents know there is a meeting at all. Those are the parents who need contact with me the most because their kids are probably going to have problems with school.

August 24

After collecting the vocabulary from all my classes, it is clear to me that my seniors are going to be lazy. On 50% of the papers I cannot even read their names. On an assignment that requires that you spell all the words correctly when the words are on the worksheet in front of you, half of them misspelled so many that they ended up with F's. After I spell check their work, we correct the answers together in class and that means if they did not spell correctly on the answer sheet, that they are still going to be losing points when they correct their papers. They have to look up eleven words on their own to start the assignment and even that seems to be a burden for them. We ran out of time in class because we were trying to cover all the preliminary things and didn't have time to drill at all.

August 25

Last day of the week. Whew! What an exhausting week. It is always that way, but especially bad because of the sheer numbers.

Reflections: This year I am hoping kids don't turn in work because of the overwhelming aspect of correcting it. That is a real dichotomy because my sessions with parents is instructing them on how they can check to see their kids get their work done. But the load is so heavy; I even had second thoughts about meeting with parents. I feel like thanking kids if they don't turn work in.

August 28, 2000

Today went well. I explained to the kids that I was giving them a gift by allowing them to make up a test if they received a D or F. I said if they did not make the effort to make up the work, it would be a sign that they didn't care. I explained to them that they all knew that no one could force them to do the work. It lies with them in terms of desiring to do it. However, I explained to them that if they gave a gift to someone and they threw it on the floor and stepped on it, would they want to give the gift again. I hope I made my point.

Also, early last week, I gave everyone my phone number and told him or her to call if they had a question about anything. I remember learning how to do computer programs this summer and not having anyone I could call to access information and how frustrating that was. I am trying to place the burden on students and parents to call me so I don't spend hours on the phone. I called several kids last night to encourage them to make up the test, and one father said I should not call on Sundays. He said I should be able to take care of any business during the week. Today when I talked to the daughter, he never even told her I called. She was embarrassed that her dad was so rude. I was calling to let her know that she should study on Sunday so she could retake the test on Monday. He never said a word to her. Getting called on the carpet makes me angry and makes me want to never call another parent again. It was like last year during mid-year parent/teacher/student meetings when two mothers blew up at me for trying to get them to come to my meeting. You never know what you are going to get with parents, or where they are coming from in terms of their own background, ignorance, or lack of respect for me and/or education. It's a mystery that parents can blame me for trying to forge a partnership with them to help their son or daughter.

August 29, Tuesday

Regular routine and that night I had about 15 parents show up for the meeting. It went really well. Since all the kids have their planners now and the parents know, I think we will see some improvement in study habits.

August 30, Wednesday

All day I took my kids to the theatre to have the rules discussed. It was great for me because I had a chance to correct all my homework. I had another meeting that night and about the same number showed up. Parents were very supportive.

August 31, Thursday

Review day, along with clarifications of a number of general rules about homework and the manner in which to do certain things. I had to talk very fast in order to get the review done and I still didn't have enough time. Encountered my first two cheatings. I lectured the kids about cheating and being dishonest in my class the first week. Two kids had identically typed homework but with a different name at the top. The biggest mistake a kid could make is this one because an enfant could tell they are a copy of the same thing. I immediately called the kid whose parent I had met the week before. This was the first great test for meeting parents. Since we had already met, I felt comfortable with her. I explained what I had discovered and she related what she knew, then had me call her son to ask him. This is what happened. The night before he had typed his assignment, but his printer did not work, so he took a floppy disk to school and ran it off. The bell rang, and he bolted so he wouldn't be late to class, leaving it on the screen. Apparently, the other kid came in, saw it and thought he was a golden opportunity to cheat. So, he did a five second name change, ran it off and committed his first grievous sin with me. I called his mother, but she only spoke Spanish, and I could only say a few words about not doing his studies. At any rate, I am sure she mentioned my call to him. One of my senior girls was giving me the body language of a bad attitude and I mentioned that things were very hectic this week, but that things would calm down next week and after class I went over to her and assured her it would get better. She said she didn't care because she was getting out of my class anyway. I asked why, and she said she didn't like the way I ran my class. Oh, well, with 40 kids, I thought good riddance! Sometimes, it is hard to get out so she may just be stuck. Then the Assistant Principal said they were trying to create a new senior section and would have to move some kids anyway. That is usually done by lottery. They should let kids go who want to go. Now I may lose some kids whose parents I have already met and the parents will not like that either after having met me. Most parents like what I have to say and they are now informed of how I do things and it would mean their kid has to go to someone entirely different.

September 1, Friday

I showed the papers to each class and explained why cheating was a really stupid thing to do. I told them what the consequences would be. I would call their home, write them up, give them a zero on the work, and it would go on their records permanently. Another incident occurred where one kid copied another's and on both papers the same exact words were misspelled. I wrote a note on their papers to see me. The kid who gave the work apologized and said it would never happen again. The kid who cheated came up to me the next day, (probably after the other kid told him to see me) and explained that he had copied. I told him because he owned up to it; I would give him a warning. Afterwards, the full consequences would take place. I put up four banners in the front of the room to solidify my points. They said, "Honesty: It Makes Life Easier", "Honesty is: Not Copying Someone Else's Work", "Do not Download from the Net or copy others' files", and "Do not look at other's work during a test". One of my seniors said, "See ya' in church", on the way out the door. The little snoot! It took me a moment to figure out what he meant by it, but I shall ask him next week.

Reflection: Trying to cram as much instruction in as possible, given that lousy 52 minutes, I tend to talk too fast and certain kids cannot even follow a word I am saying. I am finally realizing that kids are terribly deficient, rather than lazy in doing their work. They would do it if they had more success. They may have failed English for years and take the quickie course in the summer but really never retained what they needed to move on to the next level. They come into class with the idea that they can't do well in English because they never have, and in two weeks they are buried in work because they can't keep the pace, and the cycle goes on. This year, with the early parent meetings I hope to counter some of this. However, keeping track of the total number of parents who came and taking a look at their kids, I am able to draw some conclusions. Sixty-three parents came, out of 175. That is a record for our school because we customarily get 1-2% to turn out for our one-shot Back to School Night. I got nearly 40%! Most of those kids are doing really well right now. I will report on their progress as we march along.

Week of 5-8 September

Tuesday night I had another meeting at an earlier hour (4:30) and I had about ten more parents show up. There was a large Hmong crowd, and I had a translator here for them.

The big issue on Friday came down to me via the assistant principal. She came in to tell me that my two classes of seniors were being dropped and they were adding one more sophomore class and one junior class. She said she wanted to check with me first because I had seniority. I said I would not like to change, especially since I had met with so many parents. They had just hired a new teacher to take over sophomore and senior classes. Instead of the usual approach to the new teacher on the block getting whatever, they are now trying to give the best assignments to them and make the veterans do penance and take the shitty load. No thanks. Just because I am skilled enough to manage any hogwash they send my way, doesn't mean I have to accept it. So, I said no. They will be reducing the loads for all sophomore and senior teachers, so they randomly select those kids whose schedules will be least affected by it, and send them packing. This means a major upheaval in their schedules, and major reorganization for me. I have already put in their grades, established folders, and started accumulating extra credit points.

Reflection: It is insanity at the end of the first three weeks of school, that causes such a major upheaval. The administration knows the numbers enough to anticipate this before school starts. We are all just numbers on a printout and the numbers are manipulated until the class loads even out. However, this is not done in other schools. In Germany, there were one to two kids moved out of 150-student load within the first week, if that. It is simply madness to rearrange everyone's schedule starting the fourth week of school. They should be able to make predictions based on the yearly influx of kids and do their damage control before school starts.

Week of September 11-15

This week we had Back to School Night and I think I set a record. I had 65 parents come in. They filled up both sides of the sign-up sheet. More sophomore parents came than senior parents. I now have met with 107 parents. This is about 60 % of everyone. I had two students translating in Hmong and Spanish. I had to speak a mile a minute to complete the presentation. I felt like I had run a marathon when I was done. I sent out one last notice for this Tuesday, and it will be my last. Some parents are calling and some are coming, but my goal is to reach 90% of the parents and then follow the student and see whether it makes a significant difference in grades.

They are starting to send out students to fill up five more sections of English. I am hoping I can get my workload down. By Period 6 on Friday, I was in tears from sheer exhaustion. I stayed home while Martin went to the coast and sequestered myself in all day to read at least 100 essays. This is just too much. It looks like I may be taking off Quarter 2 for surgery, which will put a huge hole in my research. Oh well, there is nothing else to be done.

18-22 September

This week I had my last parent meeting. Only one Hmong parent showed up on time, a Hispanic parent showed up one half hour late and another Hmong parent showed up three quarters of an hour late. I had translators there, and several Spanish-speaking parents were called and confirmed coming and only one of those called actually came. I had the meeting at 5 pm and I think that is too early for those who may be farm workers and some who do not have transportation.

I also had a traumatic situation in the computer lab this week. When I asked the head librarian if she could hook my computer up so I could do a power point presentation for the kids, she said it was too hard and she did not have time to show me. I was devastated. No support in the lab is horrible. As it turned out, the kids were shuttled from the main lab where I was originally signed up two weeks before school started and some other teacher was able to usurp my position. I went from 40 computers to 25 in the library and along with that, the two systems were not matched up yet. So the kids outside the lab were on an old setup and the ones in the lab in the new setup, so kids could not work from one place to another without serious difficulties. And that's exactly what happened. I am trying to teach my subject for the computer usage while trying to put out fires. So I have literally a dozen questions and problems I am trying to solve and don't have a tech person to help. I ended up losing it in my senior class and cried, then got it under control. I am also punished for not remembering protocol in the lab, like getting kids to all log off and keeping kids out until all computers are realigned. I have not taught full time on the main campus for four years and I was trying to do a zillion different things at one time and then was hassled by the librarians for not following protocol. The head librarian finally got around to informing me about the discrepancy between the front computers and the back computers.

I had several bad days this week and finally decided to go see a shrink. This therapist is our crisis prevention counselor at the school and has her own practice on the side. I spent almost two hours with her, crying and swearing and shouting. I felt a lot better afterward. It is fortunate that she has a similar take on education. She also said that my hormonal imbalance might have something to do with the problems I have been having. I did start to take lunch off and take a break, because before I worked straight until I left at night. It is common to work a 60-hour week. The madness of coming back to school after several weeks of doing nothing is a horrible shock to the system. 'We have to hit the road running the moment you arrive at school. It is never the kids who are the problem; it is the inadequate system that fails to meet the needs of 85% of the students.

25-29 September

My numbers have dropped by about 20. Work has evened out and I had no more parent meetings. I called two parents with seniors who were failing. One parent, who did not know about any of the meetings, chewed my butt when I suggested that she ask to see her son's work and post the homework schedule on the refrigerator door. She told me not to tell her how to raise her son. She lost her husband last year and is raising four kids on her own. She works a second shift and probably has a lot of guilt attached to the fact that she can't stay on top of everything concerning her kids. She also said that "if he fucking well did not want to do his English, then he fucking well won't do it", and in the same breath she said all she cared about was that he graduated. She didn't want to hear that he needed to pass my class in order to graduate. Then she turned the tables on me and said her son had talked about me and she knew why he didn't want to learn from me. When I asked her why she said she wasn't about to tell me, and neither would he. So, after that phone call, I called another parent (glutton for punishment?) whose kid was in the exact situation. This mother had attended my meetings, and she was aware that he was failing, but she had misplaced the homework schedule and didn't know where it was. I asked her if she had posted the schedule on the refrigerator and told her I just got chewed out about calling another parent. She was swift to thank me for my extra efforts and said she appreciated it. Thereafter, I called the counselor and V.P. to inform them about the irate parent, as she requested we have a meeting. When the counselor called my student in to ask if he had a problem with me, he said no, that his mother was very sensitive about people suggesting she was not doing a good job. Then, he was transferred out of my class to avoid any future problems.

Another student, (whose parents only speak Spanish) and who had also done next to nothing, asked to be moved to another class because he said he could not keep up with my energetic teaching style. I agreed that the first two weeks are way too much for a slower student to handle. I talk a mile a minute anyway, and there is so much to cover that I can see deficient students being at a complete loss. They come in reading several grades below their level, encounter fast-talking, fast moving me, and are blown away. By the time the dust settles, they are so far behind, they can never catch up. I have at least 30% of my students in that category. Add to that, parents who don't speak the language and who don't come in for the parent meetings, and you have a recipe for failure. Now, the kid spent three days out of my room, trying to make a change. The V.P. will allow a move to be made with hardly a question asked for the senior with the irate mother, but this other kid, she has to have a conference and wait another week so he is so far behind, he will never pass the quarter. I totally understand how these kids get into that position.

I have only three weeks left to teach before my surgery. I am having a really good sub take over for me so I know she will do a good job. I am looking forward to the time off, although it will definitely mess with my research. However, I have a good indication of how it is going by virtue of the fact that I will be recording the grades for the quarter. Also, another hole in my research is losing 20 kids. I will have to figure out how many of those had their parents come and if they are able to maintain their grades.

OTHER IDEAS OF CHANGE

(EXCERPT FROM ARTICLES)

According to Superintendent Delaine Eastin, we are spending too little time in the classroom. She proposes 200 school days instead of 180. Along with that, more kids need to be attending summer school, especially kids who have English as a second language or kids who are getting behind in school (Thompson A1).

As it is, many kids who attend summer school are there to stay ahead of the game. They want to get certain courses out of the way, to allow them to take more electives during the school year or finish school earlier. In Germany, they actually attend fewer days than we do if you count the week they take off for class trips and the week they take off for class projects. The students have 13 weeks of vacation distributed at different times during the school year and two more weeks of school trips and a project, which is like being on vacation.

Eastin plans on phasing in a longer school year starting with adding two days this year. She also says that it would be a lot cheaper to have kids take a summer school class than repeat an entire school year, but at the moment, there is a cap on how many kids can attend. Apparently, California School Board Association President Jeff Horton endorsed both a longer school year and lifting the cap on summer school attendance" (Thompson A12). Since there will be more demands on students to pass the state exams, that would seem a prudent thing to do.

According to another article, "Adding Year to High School Wrong Approach" there has been some suggestion of adding a fifth year to the high school experience. ("Adding" B5) In Germany, they already do that. It is the 13th year and that is the big year of major exams. They have to take three five-hour written exams in three classes of their choice, plus one oral exam, comprised of a 30 minute preparation and a 30 minute oral response in a fourth subject. However, in the near future, there will be one class chosen by the state out of those three. Also, an oral interview is required in one other class, chosen by the student. If they do not pass all tests, they do not graduate. It is as simple as that.

The article does not agree that this fifth year will work and suggests that we simply work the kids harder for the four years ("Adding" B5). I think they need to consider what other countries are doing. It works for them, why can't it work for us? Not to mention that German students take 9—12 classes per year as opposed to the six that our kids take. The argument is that a fifth year would weaken an already weak system by giving them a longer period of time to graduate ("Adding" B5). It is like they will just goof off even more, in their estimation by giving them an extra year to catch up. I think it is fair to say that no one really has a handle on how to improve the school system. Too bad they can't look at other models in other countries without feeling like they are copping out to others' beliefs. It's the stubborn American way, I guess.

PARENTAL INVOLVEMENT
MANEUVERING THROUGH
ROUGH WATERS

It is extremely helpful, but not totally mandatory, to have parents who are committed to their child's education. That does not mean they have to possess a Ph.D., just a persistent reinforcing attitude to help keep their child on track. For some students, a strong role model in a teacher may do the trick, for others, a strong parent will be most helpful. Where there is desire to learn, there is passion and where there is passion, there is a drive to succeed and nothing can keep a person back with this attitude.

I would also have a regular contingency of parents representing all the ethnic groups attending, at every meeting that is held, regardless of the meeting. Parent representatives must be elbow to elbow with teachers to be sure that we do not shift our focus.

By the same token, students of every race and economic background need to be at the meeting. Regular input from students is vital to the success of the program. That means one black, one white, one Hispanic, one Asian, one upper class white parent; one lower class whatever parent. There needs to be an even distribution at these meetings that represent the overall community cross section. We need leaders in Hmong, Vietnamese, Spanish, Indian, whatever, to take back the information to those parents who do not speak English. There could be three or four alternating parent reps from each group, in case one or the other cannot make a meeting.

My parent meetings involve specific steps for them to follow that can guarantee success if strictly adhered to on a consistent basis. Here are the rules:

For time management and better study skills, make sure they have:

Specified time each day to study (same time & place)
Quiet place/privacy
Use of agenda (a date book is given to each student by the school)
Homework comes home every day in binder <u>with agenda</u>
Binder is neat and orderly at <u>all</u> times
Keep literature and grammar books at home (<u>if</u> the teacher has a class set in the classroom)
Homework schedule given a month in advance

In addition, parents can personally:
Ask to see homework every night
Have them transfer my homework schedule to their date book
Work elbow to elbow with them the first few times
Post homework schedule on the refrigerator door
Ask questions about their work
You don't have to understand it to check on it
Ask to see the sheets I give them with the completed work
Ask them to teach you what they have learned
Ask to see their homework every night for three weeks to establish a habit
Thereafter, ask to see it a different day once a week. Be consistent until you see good grades
Be positive, encouraging and firm
Have them call me if they have any questions or problems with the homework
Encourage them to come in for extra help or accept tutoring, which is offered after school in the library.

REFORMS
THE CHURNING SEA
(EXCERPT FROM ARTICLE)

The number of reforms that have been tried since I started teaching twenty years ago would boggle the mind. The government has pitched various programs for one reason or the other, but the conglomeration of these reforms has resulted in mass confusion by teachers, parents, and students. Administrators mindlessly follow where the state leads in order to get specified monies, but these subsidies change from year to year and without being able to follow through on one idea for 3-5 years to see if it actually works, we can never really know if it will succeed. Some of the programs that were created and then bit the dust were our Read/Write Program for deficient kids; a "B" Track for non-college bound kids; "A" Track for college-bound; Tech Prep for work-bound kids; Communication 2000 as an advanced Tech Prep; Mainstreaming Special Ed kids into regular classrooms; Collaborative Tech Prep; and then there was a proposed class size reduction, standards for each class level, state-wide standardized tests, four new programs to increase reading skills, a new test to be passed to graduate, and putting low-scoring schools (such as mine) into a three year improvement program (Herald 5/27/2000 B3). Add to this, the threat of firing non-tenured teachers and replacing administrators if these standards are not met. The other side of the coin is new proposals to increase teacher salaries, pay off their school loans, eliminate taxation, decrease more class sizes, and you have the typical year-to-year, month-to-month changes that occur in this state of California. For this reason, others are writing reports critical of school reform:

> ... The report criticizes state politicians for judging schools before the standards are fully in place and for measuring their success with a single standardized test, the Stanford 9 that is not directly related to those standards. (Herald 5/27/2000 B3)

Teachers are being held responsible for test scores on tests that do not reflect the curriculum.

> The report also emphasizes that the state's reforms have not adequately addressed the important problems of family poverty and inadequate early education. (Herald 5/27/2000 B3)

In the area where I teach this is especially true. The poverty level is acute. We have one of the highest teen pregnancy rates and only 2-4% of the entire school population goes directly to university. This is in vast contrast to Orange County, for example, that has the vast majority going on to 4-year colleges or universities right after graduation. You cannot throw us into the same stew pot with Orange County and expect to come out with any other results but to be one of the 430 low-scoring schools that the governor mandated for improvement

SENIOR FINALS
THE FINAL RACE

Seniors in a German school are in the thirteenth grade. Their finals are the determining factor for graduation and are taken quite seriously.

One week prior to exams they are given the week off to study. That means that the senior teacher could have off a number of weeks depending on the number of senior classes they have. During the exam the whole building is cleared out so that it is quiet for them to test. They must write continuously for five hours in three courses. Two are courses they have chosen as their major area of study; and one course is chosen by some other authority (which is a new rule for the upcoming year). Before, they were allowed to designate the subject area for the third course. Also, a fourth course is chosen for the oral interview.

Normally 2 teachers must read these 20 page dissertations before a final grade is given. If one of the teachers does not agree to passing this student, a third teacher comes in to read. Only after passing all four exams are they considered for graduation. After they pass these exams, the rest of the year is just regular classes, but they still need to maintain good grades for wherever they end up going afterwards. So, essentially, at the beginning of the second semester is when they take their exams. Exams last over a two-week time period. That's also the reason that twelfth grade is so critical because they must be preparing for the intensity of the finals.

"SENIOR SHIT DAY"

Seniors also have what they call Senior Shit Day. It is a secret day whereby they wreak havoc in the school for the first two periods. They may mess up the instructor's car or paint the windows or scatter things all over the stairs to barricade it from the teachers. They also put out a special edition of a newspaper where they complain about all the things wrong with the school or pick on teachers that were not well liked, talk about field trips, weekend excursions or what they liked about certain teachers. They would also have photos of events and people, similar to the yearbook in American schools, but on a much smaller level.

SEX EDUCATION
WHAT'S BURIED IN THE SAND?

Let's start by looking at what the Germans do. In Germany, students begin to learn about sex in the fourth grade. Each year, thereafter, they add a bit more. In fact, in the eighth grade, students give oral presentations on different types of birth control. For example, giving a demonstration in how to use a condom and showing the various kinds of condoms on the market. Parents are very open about it and as soon as they hear that their daughters are interested in young men, they have them take birth control pills. Sex is treated as a natural part of life, and is faced with the proper precautions that discourage teen pregnancy, HIV, and other venereal diseases. In my opinion, I think religion (or the lack thereof) has something to do with it. Northern Germany does not have as strong of religious ties like Southern Germany, where Catholicism predominates. Therefore, the guilt issue does not seem to interfere with the educating of their youth. I can only speak for the northern part of Germany because I have spent only minimal time in the south. I did talk to a few northern German mothers of teenage girls and they were quite frank about their straightforward approach. In fact, many kids have sex at home because parents believe they should have the privacy of their own rooms to pursue what they choose. They feel that it is better to do it at home, in the comfort of their own rooms so that they don't end up in the back seat of a car and let things get out of control. Furthermore, condoms are readily available everywhere. The relationships between mother and daughter are quite close, as I observed it, and there tended to be no big secrets, especially about sexual issues. Many German couples end up living together before marriage or not marrying at all. This includes having children out of wedlock if they have been together for several years. Most German couples do not want to have children before 25 and they usually don't.

In America, sexuality is a big issue. In the Hispanic community, it is especially difficult because of the strong Catholic upbringing. Sex is totally taboo, and as a consequence, naturally, we have a very high teenage pregnancy rate. Since mothers do not talk to their daughters about it, except for saying it is bad or forbidden, if at all, young girls tend to mess up their life at an early age. Also, since so many Americans are deeply religious, they are plagued by guilt if they even think about it. There is no realistic approach to the issue, so the problem never resolves itself. Furthermore, some parents do not want the schools to touch the subject and you customarily have to get permission for kids to see explicit films or hear speakers talk about the subject.

"SCHOOL SUCKS"

That's what most kids think
While they twirl their pencils idly

"This stuff is so boring!"
Quips another.

"Can we watch movies today?"
They whine

"How about canceling class and having a pizza party?"
Interjects a normally reticent kid in the back row

"Shut up, Stupid, we have to get ready for the test!"
Retorts one of the few "100% plus" students

"Do you have to use the "S" word?" scolds the teacher.
"Can't you at least think of a <u>different</u> adjective to use?"

"Afternoon in School:

The Last Lesson"

When will the bell ring, and end this weariness?
How long have they tugged the leash, and strained apart
My pack of unruly hounds: I cannot start
Them again on a quarry of knowledge they hate to hunt,
I can haul them and urge them no more.
No more can I endure to bear the brunt
Of the books that lie out on the desks: a full three score
Of several insults of blotted pages and scrawl
Of slovenly work that they have offered me.
I am sick, and tired more than any thrall
Upon the woodstacks working wearidly.

And shall I take
The last dear fuel and heap it on my soul
Till I rouse my will like a fire to consume
Their dross of indifference, and burn the scroll
Of their insults in punishment?—I will not!
I will not waste myself to embers for them,
Not all for them shall the fires of my life be hot,
For myself a heap of ashes of weariness, till sleep
Shall have raked the embers clear: I will keep
Some of my strength for myself, for if I should sell
It all for them, I should hate them—
—I will sit and wait for the bell.

D. H. Lawrence

SPORTS
A RACE TO THE FINISH

In America, sports programs are very big. We offer dozens of sports for students. Most sports have freshmen, junior varsity, and varsity levels. Fall starts with football, which is one of the most popular sports. Practice starts in the summer and continues until the end of the season in November. This means every day there is a 2-4 hour workout, with games played on Fridays, both at home and away. When a football kid is playing, he can be tied up with the game 15-30 hours during the week. For an away game, including travel time there and back, and depending on how far away it is, they may not return until midnight from the Friday game.

Coaches are an integral part of every athlete's life. Coaches are dedicated beyond the norm because the time is put in over and above their regular teaching position. Coaches can be the best role models or holy terrors. It all depends on how personally committed they are to winning. For every student who participates, they learn teamwork, discipline, and dedication. I feel it is an excellent experience. However, their academic work is bound to suffer, unless they are already an excellent student. It is a lot of pressure to put on kids to expect them to excel at sports and academics equally. Sometimes, athletes are exceptional at sports and terribly deficient academically. That's when the compromise takes place. Coaches have been known to bargain for grades. In some cases, it may be to get the superstar extra help; in other cases, it may be to have a grade changed so they are still eligible to play in the final playoffs for season superiority. Imagine having a winning linebacker who has kept the team on a roll right up to the final game and he is flunking out of a class that pulls his GPA below the acceptable mark to play. He becomes ineligible and jeopardizes the playoffs. That's a hard pill to swallow for the kid and the coach.

During the fall, there is also girls' volleyball, boys' and girls' water polo, boys' tennis and track; in the winter, basketball for boys and girls at all levels, and wrestling for boys; in the spring: soccer, baseball, swimming/diving, track, golf for all kids and all levels, and girls' tennis. We have a large number of kids involved at one time or another, and some of the super jocks play sports all seasons. It is a huge commitment, especially if there is the scholarship possibility, sometimes worth $200,000 for a four-year college. One year, one of my super jocks was failing English just before graduation. He had already been accepted into a private four-year college with full tuition ($200,000), but he wasn't going to graduate from high school without passing my course in English. His grade was close to passing, so I gave it to him. As it turned out, the academic program was too rigorous for him and he dropped out, thereby losing that chunk of tuition money. Another colleague of mine had a football kid who wasn't passing English the latter part of his senior year, and he committed suicide over it. Sports are a serious matter in American schools.

In German schools, sports play a smaller role. There are not as many to choose from and interschool playing is nonexistent. Most sports are played through town sports clubs who participate with each other on their own time. Germans feel that academics need to remain that way, with no interference from a heavy sports schedule that requires so much time from a kid.

STARTLING STATISTICS

School by the Numbers

7,000

. . . students drop out of high school every school day, for a total of about 1.3 million students a year.

12%

. . . of U.S. public high schools (about 2,000 schools) produce nearly half of the nation's dropouts and 58% of African-American dropouts.

50%

. . . of incoming ninth graders in urban, high-poverty schools read three or more years below grade level.

39%

. . . of high school students reported spending one hour or less a week reading or studying for class in 2009.

23%

. . . of new American teachers come from the top third of their graduating class.

14%

. . . of new American teachers in high-poverty schools come from the top third of their college class.

100%

... of teachers in Singapore, South Korea and Finland come from the top third of their college class.

Sources: Alliance for Excellent Education, High School Survey of Student Engagement, McKinsey & Co. 2007

TECH PREP
WEATHERING THE SURGING WAVES

Some time back, the government decided that students should learn more practical aspects of the work world and they provided quite a bit of funds to begin a program of study called Applied Communications. I volunteered to pilot the program with some of my seniors. After teaching the class for one year, I trained my colleagues to teach the same materials. It was accepted with mixed feelings, and some practiced it and some did not. Two separate sets of materials were purchased to use with the kids. It was designed to combine literature with practical everyday kinds of problem solving to get an idea across. We did a lot of simulations, role-playing, and mini projects. I even taught it at the junior college with adults who thoroughly enjoyed it because it involved so many aspects of the human condition, applied with practical applications of things done in the work environment. They even set up a program director in the junior college that coordinated programs between the college and the high school. This bulldozed its way into the classroom for about three years before the funds died out and so did the grandiose plans. The materials now sit collecting dust in my classroom, and even I have lost interest in pursuing it. It was much closer to the idea of work-based activities, but we were still trying to fit a round idea into a square format. It just wasn't working.

Our programs would get fired up and flame for a while, but eventually die because there were never enough concrete threads attaching the idea to a major plan. A plan that wouldn't crash and burn on the way to the drawing board.

UNFINISHED BUSINESS

We trudge to school each day
Teacher & student
Locked in a subliminal bind
Both suffering frustrations
Not of our own design

We want our voices to be heard
Above the din of school bells
And intercom announcements
We want to be included
Not given pronouncements

Until our voices can be heard
In every day and every hour
Until our minds can be other than emptiness
Bending to others' discernments
We have unfinished business!

VOCATIONAL TRAINING
GOING WITH THE FLOW

I once taught in a school in New Hampshire that had a really great vocational school in the next town. When students from our school reached the eleventh grade, they went to our school in the mornings and were bussed over to the vocational school every afternoon. They had some great programs there. Wood and metal shop, auto mechanic, day care, nursing, plant science, and quite a few other subjects.

In California, we only have regular high schools that try to provide vocational classes. Our usual classes are wood, metal, auto mechanic, and CAD, which is a computer drafting class. However, that is the extent of it. In fact, in the school where I was, we did not have auto shop, but most high schools do. The one shining example of a vocational school is the agriculture department, which I have outlined in another chapter. That model would be great duplicated in several other forms to include the other areas of interest to high school kids.

We continue to build new high schools, but what we really need are vocational schools that would serve as a segue between high school and junior college or other voc tech schools. However, as I have mentioned before, we could use the junior colleges to help build the bridge between academics and vocations.

WE THE PEOPLE: A MELTING POT

We the people of the United States of America represent a multitude of ethnic backgrounds, religions, and cultures. We are the Melting Pot of the World, and in many ways, a shining example of how to live in peace with acceptance of this type of diversity. Not one American can claim to have come from America directly . . . even the Native American Indians were thought to have come from Asia originally. We all possess the immigrant experience, even though some of us have generations of American born heritage. The fact is that our families all originated from somewhere else in the world. It is important to remember our heritage and to understand what a huge transition it is to come to the New World, leaving behind all that we knew from our past. The Hmong population are some of the most recent immigrants to come here and their stories will help you to recall what you might have heard from distant relatives who have repeated your own immigrant stories. Let us not forget the trials and tribulations suffered by all those who came before us. Here is a perfect example of one such culture.

I have read many essays written by my Hmong students over the last eight years—essays that poignantly portrayed the memories of those Vietnam years as related to them by their parents. It is a heart-rending story of their transition to a new and vastly different culture.

I have taken those stories and stored them in my heart, imagining that I am that head of the family who has endured the trials of their generation. Here I speak from a Hmong father's point of view:

WE ARE HMONG

Our roots lie deep
In the rich, fertile soil of Laotian hills
Where our soul was one
With the spirits of the earth

Gently, over the years
Verdant growth took place
As we created quiet villages
Among whispering brooks
And our self-sufficiency made us strong

The stalk of our growth was hearty
Well planted and tended with care
We were a quiet, peaceful nation
A nation unto ourselves

Then came the distant thunder of war
As we awoke to the sounds of screaming
Our babies
Our wives
Ourselves

A furious band of angry men
Tore down our villages
Raped our women
And killed our children

We desperately departed our loving roots
Escaping into the night . . .
Jungles & heat
Starvation & brutality.

The Mekong swallowed our loved ones.
Babies could not cry or they would die
As we lay hidden
In a distant jungle hideaway,
Our roots dangling weakly around our feet

We stumbled and fell and fought
Our way out.
Only to be horded into refugee camps,
Half dead, families torn to shreds . . .

We waited and waited . . .
For our destiny

One day, big silver planes
Came gliding into our lives
As we shipped load after load of our people
Into the beckoning skies
Our roots still wrapped around our feet
Weary & weeping,
We climbed out of Our World
Into Your World.

Great expanses of cement
Replaced our verdant fields
Our quiet hamlets supplanted by bustling cities
Noise assaulted our senses!

Now, our children leave us each day
To enter a different world
To move further away from our culture . . .
Our roots.

Because our country was taken away
We felt more pain than ever.
Our culture
Our life
Our homes . . .
All destroyed.

We hesitate to speak
We try to relate, but . . .
Our children now grow their roots in foreign soil.
But we cannot shake the Laotian soil from our feet

WE ARE HMONG

Innocent victims of a cruel war
Our roots do not grow well here
But we must fertilize it
With new ways
New customs
New traditions . . .

Yet our souls still return
To the Laos of our birth

WE ARE HMONG

XYZ'S OF EDUCATION

We started the alphabet
A long time ago

So how do we know
Where our education will go?

We learned our numbers
And time tables too

And something about
Our history in school

Then science and math
Hit us real hard

While nouns and adjectives
Were better than the Bard

We are about to exit
Our school right now

But I am still in the dark
Of just when and how

For something is missing
In this education of mine

Could it be the XYZ's
That I'll never find?

Could it be that
They forgot I'm a kid

With thoughts, feelings,
And desires instead?

That I have skills that no one has tapped
That I feel good when I know where I'm at

That I may not win any race that I know
But I know a lot about how I've been shown

I've been run round the school
In a veritable whirr

Chasing my rainbows and
Making a stir

But no one has shown me
The right path for me

Because college is not what I seek

I want to do what others have not
It is my soul that I have sought

Perhaps this is the last chance to see . . .
So why won't you help in my search for me?

YOSEMITE PROJECT
MANNING THE SHIP TOGETHER

"Win a free trip to the 2001 Yosemite Winter Literary Conference!" This was on a flyer in my box at school and it was the beginning of a journey that has resulted in a one-of-a-kind opportunity to work one-on-one with a student of mine.

Aaron LeQuia transferred into my class just after second semester began. I asked him if he was interested in doing the project with me, and he readily agreed. We would end up winning a free trip to this conference by doing a power point presentation together. The flyer said:

> Submit a creative piece consisting of no more than 250 words expressing the relevance of the Sierra Nevada to the people of California. The piece need not consist of purely written material. A panel of judges from the Yosemite community will choose the winning entry on the basis of creativity, enthusiasm, teamwork and quality of the submission.

We ended up submitting six slides depicting "A Spiritual, Philosophical, and Realistic Approach to the Sierra Nevada". The project started by asking Aaron to find information on the Net. He dug up quotes from John Muir and Thoreau and found out more about the Miwok Indians. We then divided up the writing. I wrote about the spiritual and realistic parts, and he wrote about the philosophical aspects of it, covering Thoreau and the Miwok Indians. We then edited it together, put it into the power point format, adding color, movement, graphics, and sound, and then emailed it to the committee for review. The process took about 12 hours as each slide had to be agreed upon and a great deal of experimentation went into it. We sat elbow to elbow for hours on end to hammer out the right approach. Our efforts paid off, as we won a four day trip to Yosemite February 25-March 1, 2001. The trip was worth $2000.00, and we learned a tremendous amount while we were there. We not only listened to a number of contemporary authors, like Francisco Alarcon, Gerald Haslam, Terry Tempest Williams, Al Young, and Brenda Hillman, but also wrote and photographed our way through the whole conference. We took four cameras with us and produced a follow-up presentation comprised of 48 slides with 46 of our own photos and poetry to coordinate with the photos. We spent another 60 hours on that, and presented it to the school board. It was the culmination of one of the best teaching experiences of my career. Student and teacher equally sharing in a project; not just the teacher correcting a student's project.

ZEBRAS ARE DIFFERENT TOO

When God made the Zebra
He had a basic scheme

He knew that horses weren't the same
He wanted some with crème

He wanted some with black and brown
He wanted some with tan

He even liked the golden ones
And white ones like the sand

And reddish hues were pleasing him
His face shined like the sun

I think he really liked them all
He sure was having fun

But as He added colors here
He knew that one was missing

He knew that some horses didn't relate
He knew that some were not to mate

He knew that some were filled with fear
He knew that some held people dear

He knew that some were slow to learn
He knew that some might be spurned

He knew that some would ride alone
He knew that some would not go home

He knew that some would jump the fence
He knew that some were far too tense

He knew that some held up their head
While others kept it down instead

So, thinking of this special kind
He made the Zebra in his mind

He made the Zebra with a pen
He made the Zebra born to win

He knew the colors were the best
Both white and black put to the test

A nice striped horse is what he sought
He did not think it was a lot

So on He worked till the end of day
To make a Zebra in a special way

It's black and white to make us think
For God wouldn't make a Zebra pink!

He wants the horse to be half and half
Not just alone to make us laugh

But to recognize the spark in all
When we hear our spirits call!

Despite the fact that this research is now 13 years old, not much has changed in the public education arena. We are laying off teachers by the dozens in most school districts, which means bigger class sizes than ever before. Unfortunately, all of the problems outlined in this book still exist. Having stayed in touch with my colleagues who are still teaching, I am familiar with the issues that they still deal with everyday. It is time to take matters into our own hands and use the examples from other countries to enhance the public education experience here.

If not now, then when?

WORKS CITED

Brockway, Cindy. "Maine School is Model for Future". Portsmouth Herald. 15. February, 2001.

Darling-Hammond, Linda. "Using Standards to Support Student Success". Restructuring Brief. California Professional Development Consortia #15, November 1998.

Hall, Edward T. & Mildred Reed. "Hidden Differences: How to Communicate with the Germans". Stern Magazine. 1983.

New York Times Editorial. "Adding Year to High School Wrong Approach". Monterey County Herald 8 July 2000, B5.

Stanley, Dr. Thomas J. "A Note to the Class of 2000 and Parents". Monterey County Herald 28 May 2000, F4.

"Study Raps 'Jigsaw Puzzle' School Reform". Merced Sun-Star 27 May 2000, A4.

Thompson, Don. "State Chief Wants Longer School Year". Monterey County Herald 13 June 2000, A1& A12.

"UC Regents Approve Dual Admissions Policy". The Monterey County Herald 19 July 2001, B4.